ALDUS PHOTOSTYLER 2.0

Aldus PhotoStyler SE Tech Support

When you register your copy of Aldus PhotoStyler Special Edition, you become eligible to:
- **Purchase the full-featured PhotoStyler at a reduced price**
- **Buy other Aldus products at reduced prices during special promotions**

For assistance in using PhotoStyler Special Edition, please contact Aldus Technical Support at (900) 555-2201 Monday through Friday from 7 a.m. to 5 p.m. Pacific Time. Each call costs $2 per minute and will be charged to to your phone bill.

ALDUS ALSO OFFERS THESE FREE SUPPORT SERVICES:

AutoTech (206) 628-5728

The automated problem-solving system is available 24 hours a day.

FaxYI (206) 628-5737

The fax information system containing a library of documents on a wide range of technical information and tips for using Aldus products.

CompuServ

Access technical support in the PUBLIC sections of the ALDUSFORUM (type "GO ALDUSFORUM" at system prompt). ALDUSFORUM is staffed by trained personnel to handle basic technical questions.

For more information about Aldus products and services in the United States and Canada, call Aldus Customer Service at (206) 628-2320.

Aldus Corporation
411 First Avenue South
Seattle, WA 98104
U.S.A.

ALDUS

Aldus International Subsidiaries and Authorized Distributors
North America, Pacific, Asia, Middle East, Latin America, Caribbean

For registration, technical support, product information, or product upgrades, please contact your local Aldus subsidary or authorized distributor.

NORTH AMERICA
United States/Canada
Aldus Corporation
411 1st Avenue South
Seattle, WA 98104-2871

Tel: (206) 628-2320
Fax: (206) 343-4259 (for
technical support only)
Fax: (206) 343-3360 (other)

PACIFIC
Australia
Residents of Australia may either send their registration cards by fax or use the postage pre-paid envelope.

Aldus Software Pty Ltd
P.O. Box 672
18-20 Orion Road
Lane Cove, NSW 2066

Tel: 02-418-8488
Fax: 02-418-8489

New Zealand
Renaissance Software Ltd
P.O. Box 24-185
Royal Oak
Auckland 1030

Tel: 09-525-0702
Fax: 09-525-2383

ASIA
Hong Kong
Gilman Business Systems
22nd Fl. Tai Yau Bldg.
181 Johnson Road
Wanchai

Tel: 833-7628
Fax: 838-5372

SiS International Ltd
Rm. 301, 3/F Eastern Harbour
Centre
Hoi Chak Street
Quarry Bay

Tel: 565-1682
Fax: 562-7428

India
For the Macintosh:
Raba Contel (P) Ltd
Adhitam Kendra (FORE)
18-B Qutab Institute Area
New Delhi 110 016

Tel: 11-686-3901
Fax: 11-686-3291

Indonesia
P.T. SiStech Kharisma
JI IR H Juanda IV, No. 3B-C
Jakarta 10120

Tel: 380-7668
Fax: 380-7640

Japan
Aldus K.K.
N.E.S. Bldg. 22-14
Sakuragaka-cho
Shibuya-ku Tokyo 150

Tel: 03-5458-6735
Fax: 03-5458-6753

Malaysia
SiS International Sdn Bhd
28 Jalan SS 26/6, Taman Mayang
Jaya
47301 Petaling Jaya, Selangor

Tel: 703-9276
Fax: 703-1231, 703-1232

Philippines
For the Macintosh:
**Distributed Processing Systems
Inc. (DPSI)**
Don Chua Lamko Bld.
H.V. dela Costa corner Alfara St.
Salcedo Village, Makati
Metro Manila

Tel: 2-818-9321
Fax: 2-817-4804

SiS Technologies Phil. Inc.
G/F Tucor Bldg.
2288 Pasong Tamo Ext.
Makati, Metro Manila 1200

Tel: 2-863-996/863-026
Fax: 2-810-8022

Singapore
SiS Technologies Pte Ltd
20 Maxwell Road #11-07/23
Maxwell House
Singapore 0106

Tel: 225-9898
Fax: 222-4512

Diversitec
396th Avenue
Level 2, Guthrie Building
Singapore 1027

Tel: 468-3888
Fax: 469-8193

South Korea
InfoTech
4 Fl, Dae Yong Bldg
16-58, Han Gan-Ro 3 Ga
Young San-ku
Seoul, 140-013

Tel: 02-070-0600
Fax: 02-703-1933

Taiwan
For the PC:
Acer Sertek Inc.
11-15 Fl., No. 135, Sec. 2
Chien Kuo North Road
Taipei, 10479
Taiwan, R.O.C.

Tel: 2-501-0055
Fax: 2-501-2521

TechStar Co. Ltd.
1F, No. 5 Alley 6, Lane 303
Nanking E. Road, Sect. 3
Taipei
Taiwan, R.O.C.

Tel: 2-715-5660
Fax: 2-715-5653

MIDDLE EAST
INGRAM MICRO
Export Department
1600 East St. Adrew Place
Santa Ana, CA 92799
U.S.A.

Tel: (714) 566-7890
Fax: (714) 566-7885

LATIN AMERICA
Argentina
DNI (Distribuidora Nacional de Informatica)
Alcina 1748
Buenos Aires 1088

Tel: 541-372-5460/476-1443
Fax: 541-953-6824

Brazil
MultiSolucoes Software Ltda.
Av. Brig. Faria Lima 2233 - 6°
Andar
01451 001, São Paulo   SP

Tel: (11)816-6355
Fax: (11)210-6294

Chile
Axis División Software
Calderón 116
Providencia
Santiago

Tel: 235-8921
Fax: 235-7830

Colombia
Matrix Ltda.
Carrera 5 No. 80-31
Bogotá

Tel:210-3803
Fax: 210-4358

México
Enviar tarjetas registro a:
Aldus Corporation
Apartado Postal #5-395
Col. Cuahtemoc
06500, México D.F.

Megaplan S. A. de C.V.
Primera Cerrada de Xola 28
Col. Del Valle
03100 Mexico, D.F.

Tel: 687-7688 or 687-7357
Fax: 682-6807

Uruguay
Namer, S.A.
Pza. Cagancha 1368/802
11100, Montevideo

Tel: 90-4220
Fax: 92-4219

Venezuela
Macapro C.A.
C.C.C.T.
Torre C/Piso 7, Of. C-704
Chuao, Caracas 1064-A

Tel: 959-006
Fax: 261-8822

For Central America, the Caribbean, Bolivia, Ecuador, Paraguay, and Peru
Ingram Micro
Export Department
1600 East St. Andrew Place
P.O. Box 25125
Santa Ana, CA 92799-5125
U.S.A.

Tel: (714)566-7890
Fax: (714)566-7885

ALDUS PHOTOSTYLER 2.0

It's hard to imagine there's a product that could do more to make your work faster, easier, and more accurate. But there is. The full-featured version of Aldus PhotoStyler 2.0 offers creative imaging with unsurpassed productivity. Upgrade now and benefit from these features:

Enhanced file and memory handling

The option to load part of an image into memory, edit it, and save it back to the file.

Support for Scitex CT, Iris CT, and DCS file formats

An image management system for cataloging files, browsing albums, viewing thumbnails, and retrieving images

An Image Navigator for quickly moving around images

More color management and enhancement tools

Grayscale masking capability

Ruby Mask overlay for creating and editing selections using painting tools

Support for PANTONE®*, Trumatch, Focoltone, Toyo, and Dainippon color matching systems

More Kodak Color Management system device profiles

Additional color tuning and correction capabilities

Expanded filter support
Unsharp masking, solarization, vignette, mirror, point acceleration, focus, and more

2-D and 3-D special effects

The option to install more plug-in filters

Custom filters that you define

Enhanced image compostion and transformation features

Real-time previews

A Multi-Transform dialog box for previewing and applying multiple effects simultaneously

An Image Compute feature for creating advanced image composites and effects

A practice pad for testing tool effects

And more...

A quick Command palette for instant access to frequently used commands

A Sketch Overlay feature for adding art direction comments directly to an image

Wacom pressure-sensitive tablet support

Upgrade offer just for Special Edition customers!

Unleash the full power of PhotoStyler today! Contact your local Aldus distributor and take advantage of this special offer to upgrade to the full-featured version of PhotoStyler.

And remember, when you upgrade, you become an Aldus customer. That means you're eligible for benefits such as long-term and electronic service and support plus preferred access to the a world-renowned selection of publishing, graphics, presentation, and prepress software tools for Windows and the Macintosh.

*Pantone is a registered trademark of Pantone Inc.

Aldus International Subsidiaries and Authorized Distributors Listed Inside

Aldus Corporation
411 First Avenue South
Seattle, WA 98104
U.S.A.

Printed in USA

User Manual

ALDUS®

ALDUS® PHOTOSTYLER®

Version 2.0 Special Edition / Microsoft® Windows™

ALDUS® PHOTOSTYLER® Special Edition User Manual

Version 2.0 / Microsoft® Windows™

FIRST EDITION

July 1993

PHOTOSTYLER AND MICROSOFT WINDOWS

PhotoStyler operates in a graphics environment called Microsoft Windows, created by Microsoft Corporation. An extension of the MS-DOS operating system, Microsoft Windows gives a standard look and feel to PhotoStyler and all other Windows applications. To run PhotoStyler under Microsoft Windows, you need to license and install Microsoft Windows.

CREDITS

Project managed by David Peterman.
Written by David Peterman, Dan Hemenway, Janet Williams, Kristen Laine, and Sarah Benn.
Illustrated by Paul Carew, Karen McClinchey, and Julie Brockmeyer.
Designed by Chris Dahl.
Edited by Scott Dunn and Liza White.
Produced by David Butler and Karen McClinchey.
Indexed by Sarah Benn.
Proofread by Sally Anderson.
Photographs by Will Lockwood, Russ DeVerniero and PhotoDisk Inc.
This manual was created using Aldus PhotoStyler 2.0, Aldus PageMaker 5.0, Aldus FreeHand 3.1, and U-Lead ImagePals for screen captures.

Aldus Corporation
411 First Avenue South
Seattle, Washington 98104-2871
U.S.A.
Tel.1 206 622 5500

Aldus Pacific Rim
411 First Avenue South
Seattle, Washington 98104-2871
U.S.A.
Tel.1 206 622 5500

Aldus Europe Limited
Aldus House
West One Business Park
5 Mid New Cultins
Edinburgh, Scotland
United Kingdom, EH11 4DU
Tel. 44 31 453 2211

For service and support in the United States, please contact Aldus Corporation. For service and support in Canada, South America, and East Asia, please contact Aldus Pacific Rim. For service and support in Africa and Europe, please contact Aldus Europe Limited. Outside these areas, please contact your local distributor or dealer. If you purchased your Aldus software through a hardware manufacturer, technical support for your software may instead be provided as part of the system support from the hardware manufacturer.

ISBN 1-56026-246-X
Printed in U.S.A.
988-975

Contents

About Aldus PhotoStyler
Special Edition

What is PhotoStyler?

Aldus PhotoStyler is the most advanced image processing and production program available for the creative professional working in Microsoft Windows.

With PhotoStyler, you can use desktop computers to perform many tasks that just a few years ago were possible only by using manual photo retouchers, dedicated graphics computers, high-end service providers, and printers.

PhotoStyler lets you enhance any continuous-tone grayscale or color image, such as scanned photographs, clip art, video-capture images, or pictures created in illustration programs. You can retouch photographs, create images from scratch, make composites, modify images for presentations and electronic delivery, and produce color separations.

PhotoStyler saves you time and money while letting you retain creative control over your work.

Who can use PhotoStyler?

Anyone who creates printed or electronic materials can use PhotoStyler to prepare and enhance photographic images:

- Art directors or electronic publishers who work with scanned illustrations or photos.
- Desktop presenters looking for the most effective images to illustrate presentations.
- Architects and engineers integrating CAD/CAM renderings into photographs.
- Photographers who want to retouch, correct, or restore photos.
- Graphic designers or artists creating original or composite artwork or photo montages.
- Printers and service providers generating color separations.
- Medical researchers using visualization to represent data as images.
- Climatologists using satellite images for remote sensing.

New to image processing?

PhotoStyler includes a context-sensitive Help system that you can access at any time by pressing F1. For a glossary of image-processing terms, click the Contents button in the Help window and select Glossary.

Chapter 2 of this manual is a detailed self-paced tutorial that introduces you to many PhotoStyler features and processes.

New Features in Aldus PhotoStyler 2.0

Achieve consistent color from scan to monitor to final output with the Kodak Precision Color Management System.

The PhotoStyler interface gives you more information and easy access to tools and functions:

- Define your tool settings quickly with the tool ribbon.
- Monitor the memory indicator to see if PhotoStyler is using RAM or virtual memory.

Powerful new tools and features for image editing:

- Use the dodge and burn tool to lighten or darken highlight, midtone, and shadow areas independently.
- Crop and resample your images in one operation for easy placement in Aldus PageMaker 5.0 and other applications.
- Drag and drop selections between images. Or, use the clone tool to copy pixels between images.

Preview your work at almost any stage:

- View images before you open them using the expandable Open Image File dialog box.
- Test several approaches to image correction using multi-preview dialog boxes.
- With the Soft Proof… command, see how your RGB true color image will look when printed to a color output device.

Work efficiently on large images. Partial Edit lets you load only a portion of an image into memory for editing.

Maintain flexibility with industry-standard file formats:

- Open Kodak Photo CD files.
- Transfer files easily between different computers and operating systems using industry-standard file formats, including TIF and DCS, Macintosh, Scitex, and Amiga formats.
- Export images as CMYK TIFFs for process-color printing from Aldus PageMaker 5.0 or other applications.

Integrate your workflow and increase productivity with OLE 1.0 links to PageMaker, Persuasion, FreeHand, and any other program that is an OLE client.

Getting
Started

Learning PhotoStyler

You have many resources available for learning Aldus PhotoStyler. Answers to most of your questions can be found in this manual or the online Help system. If you can't find the answer to your question in either of these, you have several other sources for information.

User manual

This manual, *Aldus PhotoStyler Special Edition User Manual*, contains detailed information about installing and using PhotoStyler. Use the table of contents and index to quickly find the section that will likely answer your question.

Tutorial

If you are new to image editing or PhotoStyler, use the tutorial in Chapter 2 of this manual to get hands-on practice with many PhotoStyler tools and commands. The tutorial is modular—you can perform all the lessons from start to finish, or you can skip to those that interest you. If you are an experienced PhotoStyler user, the tutorial is an excellent way to learn about features new to this version. The tutorial begins on page 18.

The online Help window

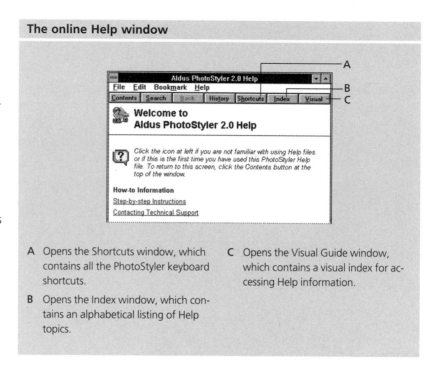

A Opens the Shortcuts window, which contains all the PhotoStyler keyboard shortcuts.

B Opens the Index window, which contains an alphabetical listing of Help topics.

C Opens the Visual Guide window, which contains a visual index for accessing Help information.

Online Help

Online Help is a powerful aid that is always available from anywhere within PhotoStyler. Simply press F1 or click any "?" button to view online Help. If you have a menu command highlighted, or if a dialog box is open, Help provides information on that command or dialog box. To learn more, choose Using PhotoStyler Help from the Help menu in the online Help window.

Fax

Aldus provides FaxYI, a free service available 24 hours a day, seven days a week. With it you can access a large database of documents covering a wide range of technical issues. Call from any Touch Tone phone and request as many as three topics per call. Request a document index on your first call to learn about all the documents available. For this service call (206) 628-5737.

Automated support

If you have a Touch Tone phone, you can call Aldus AutoTech for answers to common technical questions. It is a free service available 24 hours a day, seven days a week. The service instructs you to press keys on your phone to access the recording that answers your question. You may save your place in the system, try the suggested solutions, call back later, and resume where you left off. For this service call (206) 628-5728.

Technical support

When calling technical support, you must have your product serial number. Have paper and pencil nearby to take notes, and be prepared to restart your system if necessary. To receive technical support by telephone in the United States or Canada, call (900) 555-2201. The call costs $2 per minute and is charged to your phone bill. Technical support is available from 7 a.m. to 5 p.m. U.S. Pacific time.

Customer services

If you need to order new or replacement disks, subscribe to extended technical support, or find out about Aldus authorized trainers or imaging centers, call Aldus Customer Services at (206) 628-2320.

CompuServe

Aldus maintains a forum on CompuServe ("GO AldusForum") to answer your questions. Capable section leaders—professionals who know and use Aldus products—are available to answer your questions.

System requirements

The minimum software and hardware requirements for your computer system to run PhotoStyler are:
- a 386 processor.
- 6MB of RAM.
- a hard disk with at least 20MB free disk space.
- a VGA video card and monitor.
- a Windows-compatible mouse.
- Microsoft Windows 3.1 or later.

Boosting performance

To better handle large image files and increase overall PhotoStyler performance, you might want to consider upgrading your computer processor, RAM, hard drive, or video hardware.

Processor. PhotoStyler requires a minimum of a 386-level processor. A 486 or higher processor makes more calculations per second, thereby improving the performance of both Windows and PhotoStyler.

RAM. When you open an image file, PhotoStyler needs memory to hold the file, an undo buffer, and a working buffer. If your system lacks the necessary RAM, PhotoStyler compensates with virtual memory, which is actually space on the hard drive. Since reading from and writing to the hard drive is much slower than RAM, you can significantly improve PhotoStyler's performance by adding sufficient RAM to your computer.

To estimate how much RAM is sufficient for your work, multiply the size of one of your typical image files by three. Then add 4MB for DOS, Windows, and the PhotoStyler program. If you run other programs at the same time as PhotoStyler, you may need still more memory.

Hard drive. Since PhotoStyler may use some of your hard drive as virtual memory, the drive should have sufficient free space for PhotoStyler to create a working area. Periodically running a disk defragmentation utility increases the speed at which PhotoStyler can transfer large files to and from the hard drive.

Video card and monitor. Since low-resolution monitors and video cards cannot generate very many colors, PhotoStlyer uses a process called dithering to simulate a wider range of colors. For example, if the card can only generate 16 colors, PhotoStyler may mix—or dither—small spots of these colors to create the perception of 16.7 million colors. Although this gives the illusion of more colors on screen, the color representation is not very accurate.

For a more accurate reproduction of colors on screen, use a 24-bit color card. The 24-bit cards can display 16.7 million colors and show images (known as true-color images) without dithering. Before buying a true-color card, check the number of colors it can display at specific resolutions. For most video cards, the number of colors decreases as the resolution increases. Also, verify that the card is Windows compatible and will work with your monitor.

Before you install the software

Before you start adding the software from the distribution disks to your hard drive, take these steps to ensure the installation goes smoothly:

- Check that your computer hardware and software meet the minimum requirements.
- Verify that your computer starts and runs Windows without any errors and is functioning normally.
- Make sure your PhotoStyler package is complete.
- Make backup copies of your PhotoStyler distribution disks.
- Complete and mail your registration card.

Check the PhotoStyler package

Your PhotoStyler software package consists of the following:

- Software distribution disks
- *Aldus PhotoStyler Special Edition User Manual*
- *KODAK PRECISION Color Configure User's Guide*
- Aldus license agreement
- Product registration card, which contains the serial number

If your software is missing any of these items or you require a different disk size, please call Aldus Customer Services at 1-206-628-2320.

Make backup copies of your disks

Your license agreement lets you make one copy of each PhotoStyler disk. Before you install PhotoStyler on your hard drive, make a backup copy of each disk in the package. Use the backup disks to install the program, and store the original disks in a safe place.

To ensure the disk contents and labels are copied correctly, copy the disks using the XCOPY command with the /S switch (if working at the DOS prompt) or by choosing Copy Disk… from the File Manager's Disk menu (if working in Windows).

Register your product

Registering your copy of PhotoStyler ensures that you are notified of upgrades and other special offers. To register your copy, complete and mail the postage-paid card included in this package.

Installing the PhotoStyler software

If you have been using an earlier version of PhotoStyler, all image, pattern, and color-palette files you saved are compatible with this version.

By default, PhotoStyler 2.0 is installed in a directory called \PSTYLER. If you already have this directory on your hard drive (from an earlier version of PhotoStyler), the PhotoStyler 2.0 installer will over-write the contents of the directory. If you do not want to overwrite these files, specify a different directory for PhotoStyler 2.0 when prompted during the installation.

To install the software

1. Turn on your computer and start Microsoft Windows. Before installing PhotoStyler, be sure your computer starts and runs DOS and Windows without any errors or other problems. Turn off any anti-virus software you may have.

2. Place the PhotoStyler disk labeled Disk 1 into a floppy drive. You may install from either the A: or B: floppy disk drive. In either Program Manager or File Manager, choose Run... from the File menu. The Run dialog box appears.

3. Type a:\pssetup (or b:\pssetup) in the text box and click OK.

4. Type your name, company name, and serial number when prompted, and then click OK. Your serial number is located on Disk 2. Type the serial number exactly as it appears, including hyphens but not alphabetic characters.

5. The first time you start PhotoStyler, you should calibrate your monitor to ensure it displays colors accurately. For more information, see "Calibrating your monitor" on page 14.

6. At the end of the installation, you have the option of viewing a README file, which contains important information that was not available when this manual went to print. By taking a few minutes to read this file, you may avoid problems later.

The KODAK PRECISION Color Management System

PhotoStyler uses the KODAK PRECISION Color Management System (CMS) to bring predictable color to your computer system. The CMS is a universal color translator that interprets color between various devices, such as scanners, color monitors, and printers. With a properly configured CMS, you get consistent, accurate color through previewing, editing, and output.

A key component of the CMS is the Precision Transform (PT). A PT is a file that contains all the color characteristics for a particular device. During the PhotoStyler installation, you select which PTs you want to use by selecting the brand and model of your input device (for example, a scanner or Photo CD drive), monitor, and output device (for example, a color printer) to render color as captured in the original.

When the PhotoStyler installation is complete, the CMS compiles all the selected PTs to create a color environment that is unique to your system. As a result, the color image displayed on your screen is a more accurate representation of the output than has ever before been possible.

PhotoStyler Special Edition and the Kodak CMS

This special edition of PhotoStyler installs a default CMS configuration, but does not supply any additional Precision Transforms. Although the default configuration will produce good output results, you may want to obtain the proper PTs if color accuracy is critical to your work. To find out about the availability of PTs for your system, contact Kodak at (800) 752-6567 or by fax at (508) 670-6552.

If you change any of the devices in your system (if, for example, you decide to use a different printer), you can use the KODAK PRECISION Color Configure program to select new PTs. For more information, refer to the *KODAK PRECISION Color Configure User's Guide* included in your PhotoStyler package.

Using a default CMS configuration

During the PhotoStyler installation, you have the choice of loading a default CMS configuration. If you use the defaults, the CMS uses a set of "generic" PTs that produce good results for most hardware configurations. For the most accurate color printing, however, you must specify the exact equipment in your system. If your equipment is not listed among the available PTs, use the default configuration for the initial configuration. You may then want to contact Kodak for information about obtaining the proper PTs.

Common questions about the color management system

Why do I need a color management system (CMS)?

With a 24-bit video card, your monitor can display many more colors than even the best commercial printing press can reproduce. Without the CMS, your PhotoStyler true-color image may contain colors that cannot be printed; you wouldn't know until you actually tried printing the image. With the CMS, however, the colors on the screen are matched to the capabilities of your specified printer. Guesswork is eliminated and you significantly reduce the number of costly trial-and-error test prints. The CMS also matches your monitor to the input source (for example, a scanner or Photo CD drive) to render color as captured in the original.

Does the CMS work only if I have a color CMYK image on screen?

While it is true that the CMS controls only the appearance of CMYK true-color images, you can still access the CMS to guide you while editing RGB true-color images (since many PhotoStyler commands work only on RGB true-color images, you should

do as much image editing as possible before converting the RGB image to CMYK). Use the Soft Proof... command on the File menu to show you how the RGB image will look when converted to CMYK. For more information, see "Previewing color before you print" on page 84.

Does the CMS eliminate the need for me to calibrate my monitor?

No. There are numerous factors that can affect the performance of your monitor, and most of them are outside the control of the CMS. For example, the age of the monitor, the lighting in your workspace, the settings of the brightness and contrast controls, and the length of time the monitor has been on all affect the way the monitor displays colors. Therefore, to improve color representation, you need to periodically use the Monitor Gamma... command on the Preferences submenu of the File menu to calibrate the monitor (see "Calibrating your monitor" on page 14 for more information). For the most accurate calibration, you may want to use a separate monitor calibration device.

What aspects of my work does the CMS control?

The most noticeable benefit provided by the CMS is that it significantly simplifies the printing process. The CMS controls the advanced printing functions and usually eliminates the need to adjust the settings in the Print Options dialog box. If necessary, however, you can usually override CMS settings. As always, if you are having your work printed commercially, talk to your service provider first to determine which, if any, printer option settings you need to change.

What if my equipment is not listed among the available PT selections?

Your PhotoStyler package includes Precision Transforms (PTs) for the most commonly used equipment, but because of the large number of equipment manufacturers, it is not possible to supply PTs for every possible device. If your equipment is not listed, use the default CMS configuration for the initial installation. Then contact Kodak at (800) 752-6567 for information about obtaining the proper PTs.

What happens if I use the wrong PT?

The colors in your CMYK image on screen will not match what is printed. For example, if you use a PT for a low-end color printer, but you actually print to a high-end color printer, you get only the color range available on the low-end printer.

Right now I'm printing on a desktop laser printer, but I will eventually send my work to a commercial printer. Which PT do I use?

Always use the PT that corresponds to the ultimate output type, either for proofing or final production (for more information, see "Selecting a Precision Transform for final output" on page 80). When you convert an RGB true-color image to CMYK, the conversion is based on the targeted printer.

Do I ever need to do anything with the CMS once it's up and running?

Only if you change one of the devices (input, output, or monitor) in your computer system. To change the CMS configuration, use the KODAK PRECISION Color Configure program. For more information, see "Using the CMS" on page 12 and refer to the *KODAK PRECISION Color Configure User's Guide* included in this package.

Using the CMS

You select Precision Transforms (PTs) with the KODAK PRECISION Color Configure program to create color management system (CMS) configurations. The compiled PTs form the color environment in which PhotoStyler displays and prints color images. You run the Color Configure program from the Windows Control Panel.

With Color Configure, you can choose from the available PTs to create one or more configurations (each configuration is for a specific combination of input, display, and output devices). Although PhotoStyler works with only one configuration at a time, you can switch between configurations if you change your input or output device. All configurations stored on your system are based on the same monitor PT, though. Therefore, if you change your monitor, you must run the Color Configure program again to rebuild all the configurations.

You can alternate between the stored configurations from within PhotoStyler. If you want to compile a new configuration (you may do this if, for example, you add a new scanner to your computer system), run the Color Configure program.

For more information, refer to the *KODAK PRECISION Color Configure User's Guide*.

Choosing the correct Precision Transforms

Using the correct PTs ensures that image colors remain accurate from input to display to output. The PT for your output device is especially important as it controls how RGB colors are converted to CMYK.

You should use the output PT that corresponds to the final output type. When you convert an RGB true-color image to CMYK, the conversion is based on the color range of the target printer specified in the CMS. Any RGB color information that is outside the capability of the target printer is mapped to another reproducible color that is as close as possible to the desired color. You usually cannot convert a CMYK image back to RGB without a noticeable change in the colors. For the best results, do all of your image editing in RGB; do not convert the image to CMYK until you are ready to print.

Make a copy

If you know that one image will appear in multiple projects using different output methods, always retain an RGB true color copy of the image file. When you convert an RGB true-color image to CMYK, make sure New Image on the Convert To submenu on the Image menu is checked. Then when you need to change the final output type, you can return to the original RGB true-color image and convert to a new CMYK image, this time specifying a different PT when prompted by the convert command.

Making changes to the CMS and PTs

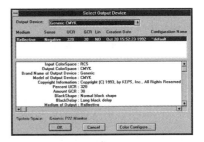

To create a configuration for your monitor and input and output devices, start Windows Control Panel and double-click the Color Configure icon. For more information, see the *KODAK PRECISION Color Configure User's Guide.*

To view or select a different input device from those you configured, click the CMS... button in the Open Image File, Save Image File, or Scanner Setup dialog box. The Select Input Device dialog box appears.

To view or select a different output device from those you configured, click the CMS... button in the Print or Soft Proof dialog box. The Select Output Device dialog box appears. This dialog box also appears when you choose CMYK True Color from the Convert To submenu on the Image menu.

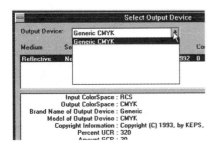

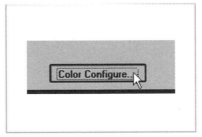

To view the characteristics of the current device, open either the Select Input Device or the Select Output Device dialog box. You can also select one of the devices you configured from the drop-down list box.

To add another PT or change one of your devices, click the Color Configure... button to run the Color Configure program again.

Calibrating your monitor

Although the KODAK PRECISION Color Management System (CMS) plays an important role in controlling the appearance of images on your monitor, it cannot compensate for all the variables that affect the monitor's performance. To ensure your monitor is correctly calibrated to work with PhotoStyler, adjust the monitor's gamma values after you install PhotoStyler and configure the CMS. Since monitor colors can shift even over the course of a few hours, you may want to check the calibration frequently (especially when you are working with color-critical images).

This calibration only affects how your monitor works with PhotoStyler; the calibration does not extend to other applications. If you place a PhotoStyler image in an application that does not display colors accurately, the image may not look the same as it does in PhotoStyler. Therefore, if you plan to display your image in another application, you may wish to skip this procedure.

Do not perform the calibration procedure if you have a 16-color (VGA) display. These displays do not show enough detail to let you adjust the gamma values properly.

About monitor gamma values

Monitor gamma values control how images are displayed on your monitor. Since each monitor is subject to a unique set of factors (for example, age, temperature, and ambient lighting), even identical models of monitors may display colors slightly differently from one another. When you adjust the gamma values, you are telling PhotoStyler how to compensate for these differences. Adjusting the monitor gamma gives you more precise RGB color representation on your monitor.

Do not confuse *monitor gamma* with *image gamma curves*. An image gamma curve is a representation of the midtone values in the image.

Before calibrating your monitor

Your immediate environment influences how you see color on your monitor. Before you calibrate a monitor, make sure your surroundings are set up as they normally are when you work:

- Make sure artificial light sources are at their usual intensity. Turn on all the lights you normally use when you work.
- Check the position of your screen relative to natural light sources. Don't face a bright window. Position your monitor to avoid reflected light.
- Set the contrast and brightness controls on your monitor to the usual working levels. If possible, mark these settings for reference.

Setting Windows desktop colors

When editing images in PhotoStyler, it's helpful to use a Windows desktop color scheme that includes only white and neutral grays. A desktop cluttered with too many colors interferes with accurate perception of the colors in your images. For more information on changing the desktop colors, refer to your Microsoft Windows 3.1 *User's Guide*.

To calibrate your monitor

1. In Windows Program Manager, double-click the PhotoStyler Icon to start the program.

2. Choose Monitor Gamma... from the Preferences submenu on the File menu. A four-part test image appears along with the Monitor Gamma dialog box. On a miscalibrated monitor, you see a block containing a different shade of red, green, blue, or gray at the center of each color block in the test image.

3. Adjust the Red value then click Preview to see how the test image is affected by the adjustment. Try to make the shade at the center of the block match the surrounding shade. Continue adjusting the value and clicking Preview until the center and outer shades in the red color block match each other as closely as possible.

4. Repeat step 3 for the Green and Blue values. When the red, green, and blue color blocks are all adjusted correctly, the gray block appears adjusted. Then click OK.

2

Exploring
PhotoStyler

Starting work on an image

Before you start the tutorial you should read Chapter 1, Getting Started, to learn how to install PhotoStyler and how to configure your computer for optimum performance. Then you can go through this tutorial sequentially or skip to a lesson that interests you.

Getting help

Whenever you want help, press F1 to access the online Help system.

Overview of PhotoStyler

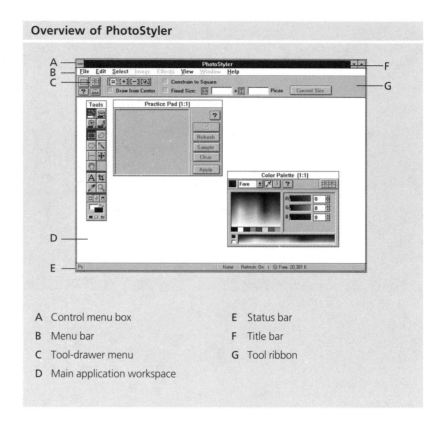

A Control menu box

B Menu bar

C Tool-drawer menu

D Main application workspace

E Status bar

F Title bar

G Tool ribbon

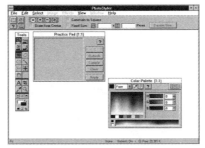

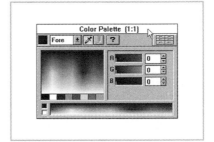

1. To begin a PhotoStyler session, double-click the PhotoStyler icon in Program Manager.

2. Click anywhere in the PhotoStyler window.

3. Press Ctrl + Shift + Z to execute the Show All command.

4. Move each palette around by dragging its title bar.

5. Clear the screen by double-clicking the title bar of each palette. Leave only the Tools palette.

Basic skills

If you've used other Windows applications, you'll feel comfortable using PhotoStyler. Here are a few more basic skills you'll use in every PhotoStyler session.

Zooming in and out

You'll learn more about zooming as you go through the tutorial. As a general rule:

- Press Z and click the left mouse button to zoom in.
- Press Shift + Z and click the left mouse button to zoom out.

Tips for preserving your work

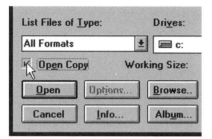

It's a good habit to open a copy of your file, keeping your original image as a backup. The Open Copy option in the Open Image File dialog box opens a copy with the name of the original image in brackets in the title bar. Throughout the tutorial, we'll refer to the copy by the name of the original file.

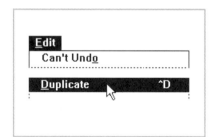

Another way to copy your file is to choose the Duplicate command from the Edit menu. This command is useful if you realize you want a copy after you've opened the original image file.

Save your file often, so you don't lose the results of your editing session. The first time you save a copy or duplicate, the Save Image File dialog box prompts you for a filename. After that, you can press Ctrl + S anytime to save the file.

If you make a mistake

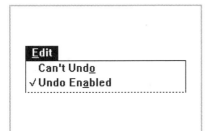

The Undo Enabled command on the Edit menu lets you undo a false move. If this command has a checkmark by it, you can undo your last action by pressing Ctrl + Z.

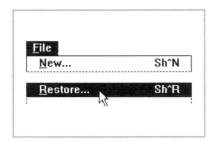

The Restore… command on the File menu restores your file or any selected portion of it to its last-saved version.

The Restore… command opens the Restore dialog box, which gives you a choice of replacing the entire image or a selected area only. You'll learn more about selections later in the tutorial.

Note: The other options in the Restore dialog box are available only in the full edition of PhotoStyler.

Opening an image file

After you scan in an image you may
need to straighten it and crop away
the scanner background before you
begin image enhancement. In this
example you will:
- open an image file.
- rotate the image to straighten it.
- crop the image.
- save the corrected image file.

Scanned-in image

After rotating and cropping

Open the image file

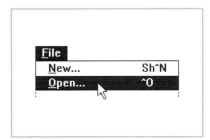

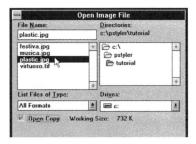

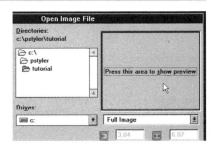

1. Choose Open… from the File menu.

2. Use the Directories list box to go to the TUTORIAL directory.

3. Select All Formats from the List Files of Type list box.

4. Click to check Open Copy.

5. Select the PLASTIC.TIF file.

6. Click Preview>>.

7. Click the preview panel to display a preview version of the file.

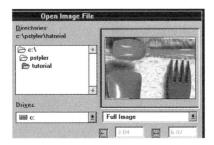

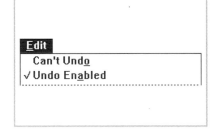

8. The image appears in the preview panel.

9. Click Open.

10. The image appears in the image window.

11. Make sure Undo Enabled on the Edit menu has a checkmark by it. Anytime you want to undo your last action, press Ctrl + Z.

Straighten the image

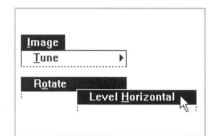

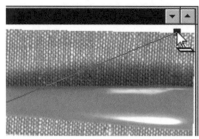

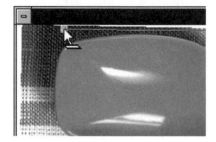

1. To prevent accidental changes to the image, select the grabber hand from the Tools palette.
2. Choose Level Horizontal from the Rotate submenu on the Image menu.

3. Position the cursor over the right handle of the rotate bar until the cursor changes. Then drag the handle to the edge of the image.

4. Drag the left handle to the edge of the image as shown above. The bar should be parallel to a line in the image you want to make horizontal—in this case the image edge.
5. Double-click either handle to apply the rotation.

Enlarge the image window

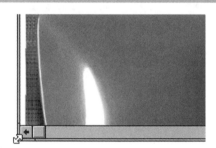

1. The image is now straight. Before you can crop the image, you need to enlarge the image window.

2. Position the cursor on the lower left corner of the window until it turns into a double arrow; then drag down and to the left.

3. The image is centered in the image window.

Crop the image

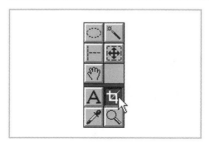

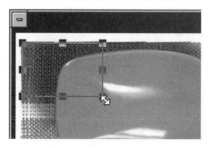

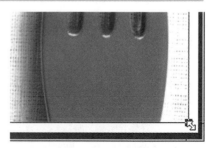

1. Select the cropping tool from the Tools palette.

2. Position the cursor over the top left corner of the image.

3. Drag the cursor to the lower right corner of the image to eliminate the unnecessary background from the scan.

4. Double-click within the cropping frame to apply the cropping.

Save the image

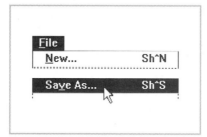

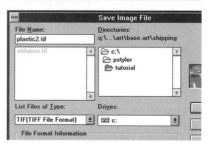

1. The image is now cropped and ready to save.

2. Choose Save As... from the File menu.

3. For File Name type PLASTIC2.TIF.

4. If necessary, Select TIF (TIFF File Format) from the List Files of Type list box.

5. Click Save.

Focusing

In this example you will focus the image using the Focus... command.

The Focus... command sharpens or softens the focus of the image. Whereas the sharpen tool increases and the blur tool decreases the distinction between neighboring pixels, the Focus... command uses the same effects to adjust the focus of the entire image or selection area.

Multi-preview dialog boxes appear when you choose commands from the Effects menu and from the Tune submenu of the Image menu. They let you compare the effects of different settings side by side before you apply them to the image or selection.

When using the Focus... command, use the Focus multi-preview dialog box to preview focus settings before you apply them to the image file.

Before focusing

After focusing

Focus multi-preview dialog box

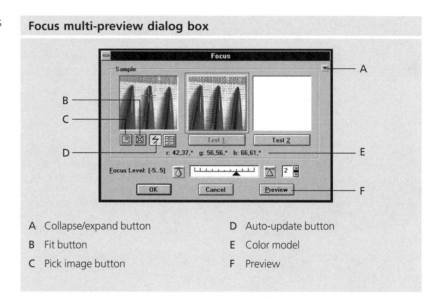

A Collapse/expand button
B Fit button
C Pick image button
D Auto-update button
E Color model
F Preview

Get ready to focus

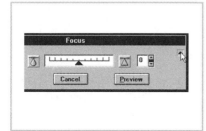

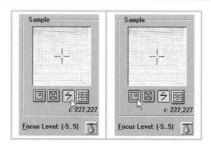

1. The PLASTIC2.TIF file should still be open. If it isn't, repeat the steps in the preceding topic to open the file.

2. Choose Focus… from the Tune submenu on the Image menu.

3. The Focus dialog box should show three preview panels. If it doesn't, click the ▲ button to expand it.

4. If necessary, click to highlight the auto-update button.

5. Click the pick image button to display the Pick Image dialog box.

6. Drag the pick box to place it over the tines of the fork. Then click OK.

Focus the image

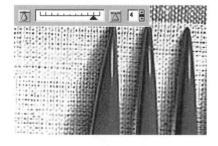

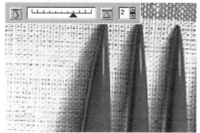

1. Drag the indicator to 4. The changes appear immediately in the Test 1 preview panel. Here the image looks overfocused.

2. Click the Test 2 preview panel and drag the indicator to 2. The effect of the setting change is shown in the active panel (Test 2).

3. This shows a more appropriate focus level. Click OK.

4. The image is now focused. Press Ctrl + S to save the image.

Adjusting color balance

In this example you will correct the color balance of the image using the Color Balance... command.

What is color balance?

An image has good color balance when gray areas look gray, neutral areas look neutral, and objects appear as they do in real life. Poor color balance is usually the result of using the wrong film or filter for the lighting conditions when the picture was taken, or of improper scanner settings.

The image you're using here has an overall blue cast to it. The Color Balance... command works like a filter on your camera lens or enlarger. To remove blue tones, you apply a filter of blue's complement, yellow. Using the Color Balance... command, you select the color "filter" you want to apply to the image or selection area to get the color effect you want.

Before adjusting color balance

After adjusting color balance

Adjust the color balance

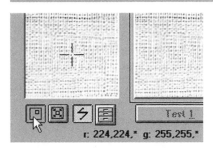

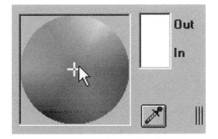

1. The PLASTIC2.TIF file should still be open. If it isn't, open it now.

2. Choose the Color Balance... command from the Tune submenu on the Image menu.

3. Click the pick image button.

4. Position the pick box over the area shown in the picture above.

5. Click OK.

6. Click the color wheel to select the color "filter" you want to apply. Unless you're going for a dramatic effect, pick colors near the center of the wheel. Since you're correcting a blue cast, pick blue's complement in the yellow-orange area.

7. Experiment with filter effects until you eliminate the blue cast.

8. When you've eliminated the blue cast and colors look natural, click OK to apply the correction.

9. The colors now look more natural. Press Ctrl + S to save the image.

Adjusting brightness and contrast

In this example you will adjust the brightness and contrast levels using the Brightness & Contrast... command.

Brightness and contrast

The Brightness & Contrast... command works like the corresponding knobs on a TV set. You adjust the settings in the Brightness & Contrast... dialog box just as you would turn the TV knobs.

About gamma values

A third function of the Brightness & Contrast... command is to adjust the gamma setting. Changing the setting on the gamma slider bar in the Brightness & Contrast dialog box from its default of 1.00 increases or decreases the brightness in the midtones of the image. Midtones are color or gray values that lie between the shadows and the highlights. On a scale of 0 (black) to 255 (white), midtone values range between about 75 and 200.

Before adjusting brightness and contrast

After adjusting brightness and contrast

If the gamma is set too low, the image is dark overall and detail is lost in darker areas.

If the gamma is set too high, colors are pale, but there is good detail overall.

Adjust the brightness and contrast

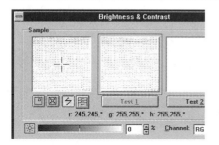  

1. The PLASTIC2.TIF file should still be open. If it isn't, open it now.

2. Select the Brightness & Contrast... command from the Tune submenu on the Image menu.

3. Click the fit button to fit the entire image in the preview panel.

4. Adjust settings in the Brightness & Contrast multi-preview dialog box:

   Brightness: 8
   Contrast: 12
   Gamma: 1.00

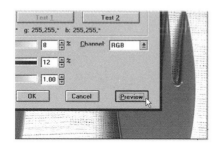 

5. Click Preview.

6. Drag the dialog box title bar to the side to view the image.

7. The brightness and contrast settings look good. Click OK to apply the change.

8. Press Ctrl + S to save the image.

Adjusting saturation

In this example you will use the Hue & Saturation… command to change the saturation of the image.

What is saturation?

Saturation refers to the intensity of a color. When colors are saturated, they appear as they would in strong sunlight; skies are clear blue, and colors of objects appear at full strength.

The saturation level you use depends on the image and on the effect you want. If an image is oversaturated, colors look unnatural and detail drops out of colored areas. If an image is undersaturated, colors are pale and weak.

Before adjusting saturation

After adjusting saturation

Adjust the saturation

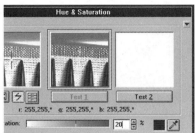

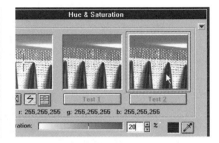

1. The PLASTIC2.TIF file should still be open. If it isn't, open it now.

2. Choose Hue & Saturation... from the Tune submenu on the Image menu. If necessary, click the ▲ button to expand the multi-preview dialog box.

3. Set saturation to 20.

4. The colors in the Test 1 preview panel look unnaturally bright.

5. Click the Test 2 preview panel.

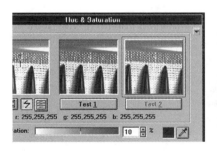

6. Set saturation to 10.

7. This setting makes the image look bright yet natural. Click OK to apply the saturation change.

8. Press Ctrl + S to save the image.

Making a selection and adjusting hue

In this example you will select an object and change its color, or hue.

Using selections

Sometimes you may want to edit only a portion of your image. For example, in this lesson you'll take one utensil in the picture and change its color. You can isolate the part you want to change by creating a selection area. Your changes apply only to the portion of the image within the selection area; the rest of the image is protected from editing. You define a selection area using selection tools on the Tools palette.

What is hue?

Hue is another word for color. When you click on the Remapped Hue bar in the Hue & Saturation dialog box, you're changing the color of the image or the portion you selected. In this example, you'll change the color of the plastic spoon.

Before changing the hue of the selection area

After changing the hue of the selection area

Selection Tools

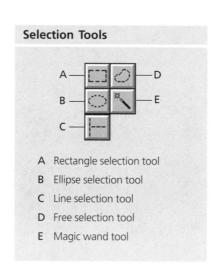

A   Rectangle selection tool

B   Ellipse selection tool

C   Line selection tool

D   Free selection tool

E   Magic wand tool

Choose the free selection tool

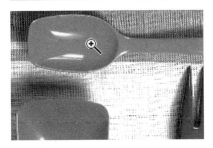

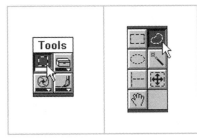

1. The PLASTIC2.TIF file should still be open. If it isn't, open it now.
2. Hold down the Z key and position the cursor on the spoon.
3. Continue to press Z and click the left mouse button to zoom in on the image. To zoom out, press Shift + Z and click the left mouse button.

4. Click the selection group button on the Tools palette.
5. Select the free selection tool

6. On the tool ribbon, specify these free selection tool settings.
   Click the = button
   Snap to Edge: checked
   Pixels: 2
   Anti-aliasing: checked

Make the selection

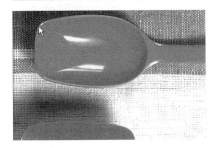

1. Position the cursor on the edge of the spoon.

2. Carefully drag around the edge of the spoon. To move in a straight line, release the mouse button, move the cursor to a new position, and click. Resume dragging for irregular areas. Don't worry about getting it perfect at this point.

3. After you've traced around the spoon, double-click to complete the selection.

4. The animated selection marquee appears. If you don't see a marquee, press Ctrl + H to turn the Show/Hide Marquee command on and off. To start over, click the right mouse button to cancel the selection.

Edit your selection area

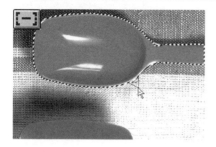 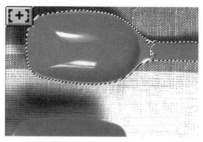 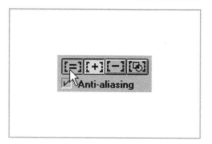

1. Uncheck Snap to Edge on the tool ribbon.

2. If you selected a little too much in some areas, click the - button on the free selection tool ribbon.

3. Make a second selection where you went wide. When you double-click to complete the selection, this area is subtracted from the first selection.

4. To add to your selection, click the + button on the free selection tool ribbon.

5. When you make a second selection, this area is added to the first selection.

6. Remember, you can always use Ctrl + Z to undo your last selection action.

7. When you are satisfied with your selection, click the = button.

Give your selection a soft edge

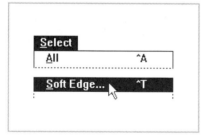 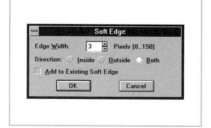

1. To make the hue change appear more natural, you can soften the edges of the selection. Choose Soft Edge… from the Select menu.

2. Specify settings in the Soft Edge dialog box:
   Edge Width: 3
   Direction: Both

3. Click OK. You may not be able to see the Soft Edge effect on the selection marquee.

Pick which color you want to change

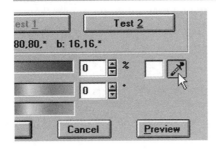

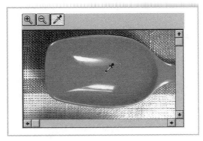

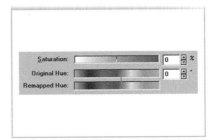

1. Choose the Hue & Saturation… command from the Tune submenu on the Image menu.
2. Make sure the auto-update button is highlighted.
3. Click the eyedropper button. The Pick a Color dialog box appears.

4. Click on the spoon.
5. Click OK.

6. A line appears on the Original Hue ribbon. The position of the line on the spectrum corresponds to the color of the spoon.

Select and apply a new color

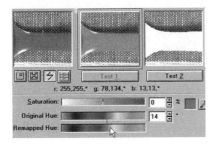

1. On the Remapped Hue ribbon, click the color you want the spoon to become. This is your "after" setting.

2. Experiment with settings, viewing the color change in the Test 1 or Test 2 preview panel.
3. When you've found a color you like, click OK.
4. Click the right mouse button to deselect the spoon.

5. Zoom out to view the entire image.
6. Press Ctrl + S to save the file.
7. Choose Close from the File menu to close the image window.

Creating a composite image

In this example you'll combine two image files into a composite image, placing the violin on a backdrop of sheet music.

Making composites

PhotoStyler offers a variety of ways to merge images together into a composite image. You can combine images using the Copy and Paste commands, floating selections, pattern files, image channels, or the Merge Control... command. In this example, you'll use the simplest method: dragging a floating selection from one image file to another.

Using the magic wand

Because the violin has a complex shape that would be difficult to trace, and because the background is all one color, you'll use the magic wand tool to make your selection. This tool selects pixels that fall within a given similarity range with respect to the pixels under the cursor. First you'll select the black background, then invert the selection to select the violin.

First image

Second image

Composite image

Open two image files

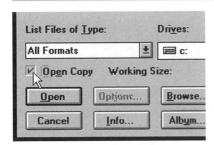

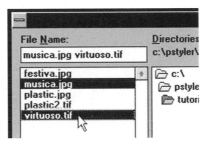

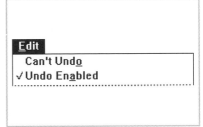

1. Choose Open from the File menu.
2. Use the Directories list box to go to the TUTORIAL directory.
3. If necessary, select All Formats from the List Files of Type list box.
4. Check Open Copy.

5. To open two image files in one step, first click VIRTUOSO.TIF.
6. Then press Ctrl and click MUSICA.JPG.
7. Click Open.

8. Make sure Undo Enabled on the Edit menu has a checkmark by it. Anytime you want to undo your last action, press Ctrl + Z. Or to restore the file to the last-saved version, choose Restore… from the File menu.

Make a selection

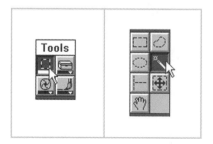

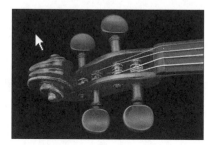

1. Click the selection group button on the Tools palette.
2. Select the magic wand.

3. Use these settings on the magic wand tool ribbon:
   Compared By: RGB
   Similarity: 5
   Anti-aliasing: checked
   = button: highlighted

4. Click on the VIRTUOSO.TIF title bar to make it active.
5. Click the black background.

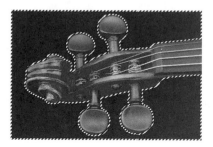

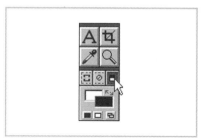

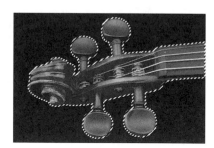

6. The black background is selected.

7. To select the violin, click the invert selection button on the Tools palette.

8. The violin is now selected.

Merge the two images

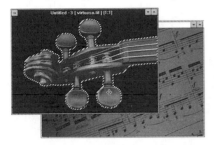

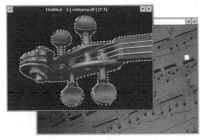

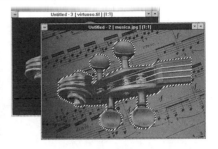

1. Place the cursor within the selection marquee; the cursor turns into a four headed arrow.

2. Drag the violin into the MUSICA.TIF image window. It appears as a small white box.

3. Release the mouse button.

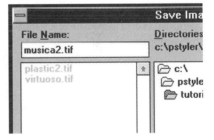

4. Drag the selected violin to position it.

5. When it's in the desired position, click the right mouse button to deselect and to merge the selection with the underlying image.

6. Choose Save As... from the File menu.

7. In the File Name box, type MUSICA2.TIF.

8. If necessary, select TIF (TIFF File Format) from the List Files of Type list box.

9. Click Save.

Retouching

In this lesson you will use PhotoStyler retouching tools to improve an image.

First you will use the clone tool to:
- remove the utility wire in the background.
- reduce background clutter to draw attention to the dancer.

Then you will use the dodge and burn tool to:
- lighten the face.
- bring out color in the arm on the left side of the image.

Before retouching

After retouching

The clone tool

The clone tool copies the pixels from one place in the image to another. You are actually painting with the contents of the image rather than with color or gray values.

When cloning, you select a source point, where you copy pixels from, and a destination point, where you copy pixels to. When you paint around the destination point, pixels are copied from the corresponding area around the source point. You can clone within a single image or between image files.

The dodge and burn tool

The dodge and burn tool works just like dodging and burning in a darkroom. Settings on the dodge and burn tool ribbon adjust the brightness in highlight, midtone, and shadow ranges. Use the dodge and burn tool when you want to restrict the effect of your editing to the area under the cursor.

The Practice Pad

The Practice Pad lets you practice with paint or imaging tools on a selected portion of the image. The effect of your editing is shown in the Practice Pad but not in the image window. After you experiment with an effect, you can:
- apply the changes on the Practice Pad to the image file.
- clear the Practice Pad of the changes and try again.
- exit the Practice Pad.

Getting started

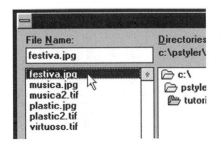

1. Choose Open... from the File menu.
2. Go to the TUTORIAL directory.
3. If necessary, select All Formats from the List Files of Type list box.
4. Check Open Copy.
5. Double-click the FESTIVA.JPG file.

6. Click the image window maximize button to expand the image window

7. The image window is now at its maximum size.

Zooming in

1. Press Z and click to zoom in to the area shown above.

2. If necessary, use the scroll bars to display the wire on the left side of the dancer.

Accessing the Practice Pad

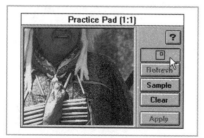

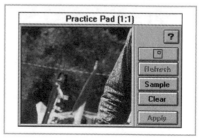

1. Press F9 to display the Practice Pad. If the Practice Pad window is blank, click the image editing group button on the Tools palette.

2. Click the pick image button.

3. Drag the square in the Pick Image dialog box until it contains the wire to the left of the dancer.

4. Click OK.

5. Any changes you make within this box on the Practice Pad you can apply to the corresponding area on the image file.

Setting up the clone tool

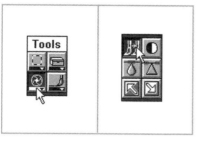

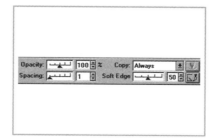

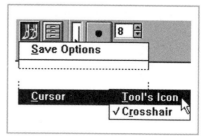

1. If necessary, click the image editing group button on the Tools palette.

2. Select the clone tool.

3. Specify settings on the clone tool ribbon:
   Opacity: 100%
   Spacing: 1
   Copy: Always
   Soft Edge: 50
   Brush: 8 x 8

4. Choose Tool's Icon from the Cursor submenu on the tool-button menu.

Clone away the wire to the left

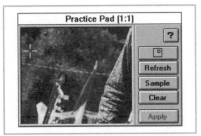

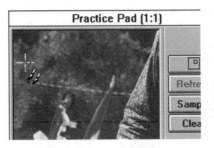

1. Within the Practice Pad, press Shift and click on the trees to set the source point. The cursor at the source point is a blinking crosshair.

2. Position the cursor over the wire and drag to clone. Note the box near the source point showing you where you are copying pixels from.

3. The pixels from the source point are copied to the area under the cursor at the destination point.

4. Continue to remove all of the wire to the left of the dancer.

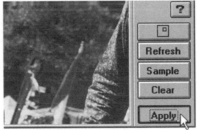

5. To undo your cloning stroke, hold down the right mouse button and drag to where you just cloned.

6. When you're satisfied with your cloning, click Apply on the Practice Pad.

7. The changes appear in the corresponding portion of the image window. Double-click the Practice Pad title bar to remove the Practice Pad from the screen.

Change the clone tool settings

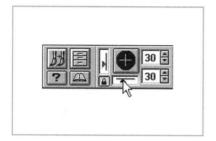

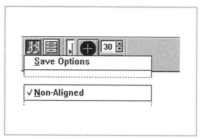

1. On the tool ribbon, change the clone tool brush size to 30 x 30. Note: When the lock button next to the brush dimensions is highlighted, the number you specify in one setting box appears in the other.

2. Make sure that Non-Aligned is checked on the clone tool-button menu.

3. If necessary, hold down the S key and drag to position the background to the right of the dancer in the image window. Note: This shortcut works only when you're zoomed in on the image.

Clean up the background

1. Press Shift and click on the trees to set the source point. You may need to zoom out to get a good source point and then zoom back in.

2. Drag the mouse over the dancers in the background to replace them with greenery. Remember to drag with the right mouse button if you want to undo your last cloning stroke.

3. Zoom out to view the effect.
4. Choose Save As... from the File menu.
5. In the File Name box, type FESTIVA2.TIF.
6. If necessary, select TIF (TIFF File Format) from the List Files of Type list box.
7. Click Save.

Reduce clutter between feathers

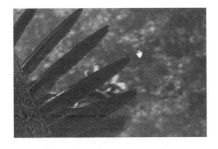

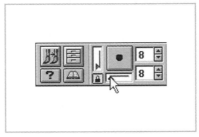

1. Press S and drag to show the feathers in the dancer's costume in the image window.

2. On the clone tool ribbon, change the brush dimensions to 8 x 8.

3. Press Shift and click to set the clone source point on nearby trees.

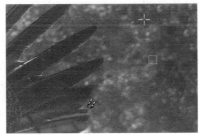

4. Position the cursor between the feathers of the costume and drag to clone.

5. Replace the background clutter with greenery.

Simplify background under the arm

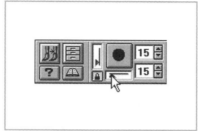

1. Press S and drag to display the dancer's right arm in the image window.

2. On the clone tool ribbon, change the brush dimensions to 15 x 15.

3. Press Shift and click on the trees to set the clone source point.

4. Position the cursor under the dancer's right arm and drag to clone.

5. Replace the background under the arm with greenery.

6. Zoom out to view the effect.

7. The simplified background draws attention to the dancer.

8. Press Ctrl + S to save.

Setting up the dodge and burn tool

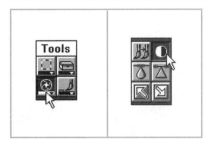

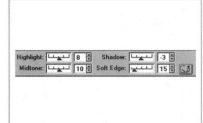

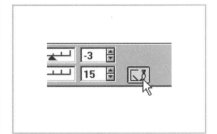

1. If necessary, click the image editing group button on the Tools palette.

2. Select the dodge and burn tool.

3. Specify settings on the dodge and burn tool ribbon.
   Brush size: 18 x 18
   Highlight: 8
   Midtone: 10
   Shadow: -3
   Soft Edge: 15

4. Make sure the continuous paint button on the tool ribbon is highlighted.

Dodge the dancer's face

1. Press Z and click to zoom in on the dancer.

2. Drag over the face to dodge it.

3. Drag with the right mouse button to undo any editing you're not satisfied with.

4. The dancer's face is now brighter and has better detail.

Burn in the dancer's arm

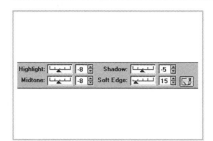

1. Change the dodge and burn tool settings:
   Highlight: -8
   Midtone: -8
   Shadow: -5
   Soft Edge: 15

2. Press S and drag to position the dancer's right arm in the image window.

3. Drag the cursor over the bright areas of the right arm and shoulder.

4. This portion of the image now appears less washed out.

5. Press Ctrl + S to save.

Scanning and Resolution

Obtaining and preparing your image

At what point do you set image resolution?

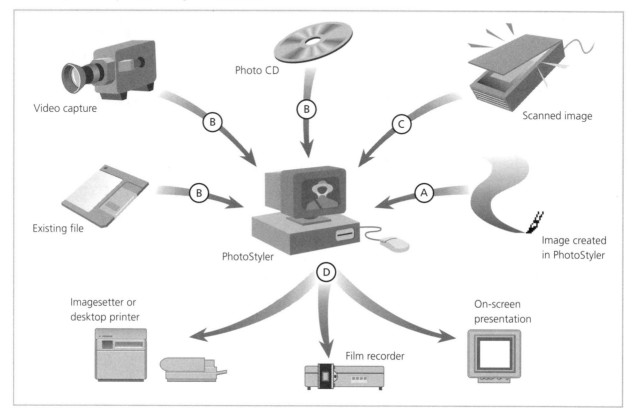

A Choosing the appropriate image resolution when you create a new image will ensure high-quality output. See topics on determining image resolution, pages 55–57.

B When you work with an existing image, you may have to adjust the dimensions and/or the resolution for your final output. See topics on determining image resolution on pages 55–57 and "Changing the size and resolution of an image" on page 60.

C When you scan a photograph, you can pick the size and resolution so you don't have to make changes later. See "Scanning an image" on page 58.

D The type of output device you will use is the primary consideration when choosing image resolution. Talk to your service provider about what equipment and medium will be used and what image resolution is appropriate. If you don't know your final output device, choose the highest image resolution possible, provided you have the required disk space, and resample later. See "Changing the size and resolution of an image" on page 60 and "Scanning an image" on page 58.

Working with PhotoStyler generally includes three stages. The first stage is getting the image into the PhotoStyler workspace by scanning, opening an existing file (from disk or Photo CD), video capture, or creating a new file from scratch. Image design and production make up the second stage and may involve correcting or altering the image.

The final stage is output—whether you want to print the image or place it in another application. Getting the best output usually requires planning before input—especially regarding image size and resolution.

If you scan an image or create a new image from scratch, you have full control over the size and resolution of the image. If, however, you are opening an existing file or a file from a Photo CD, you may need to change the size, resolution, or both to get the best output.

Consider copyright issues

Desktop scanning offers exciting possibilities for creating images, but you can't legally scan everything you see for commercial use. Here are a few general guidelines:

- Work with original material. Scan photos that you've taken or drawings that you've created.
- Before publishing a photo of a person, obtain permission from the subject of the photograph.
- If you plan to scan a photo or artwork created by someone else, get written permission from the creator or owner of the image, even if you plan to alter it significantly. Make sure you clearly indicate your plans for the image.
- If you're not a photographer, locate an agency that sells ready-to-use photographs. When you buy an image, be very clear about your usage rights.
- If you have any doubts about using an image, take time to research the license requirements. The time you spend initially may prevent legal problems later.
- These same copyright issues apply to video-captured material.
- For more information, contact the Copyright Office, Library of Congress, Washington, D.C. 20559.

What is resolution?

Resolution is the number of dots available to represent graphic detail in a given area: on a computer screen, the number of pixels per linear inch; on a printer, the number of dots printed in a linear inch; on a scanner, the number of pixels sampled per linear inch of the scanned image. In order to determine the best resolution for your image, you need to be familiar with the resolution of your output device (and any other requirements specified by your service provider).

Whether you are scanning an image into PhotoStyler, importing it from Photo CD, or creating an image from scratch, you first need to determine the appropriate resolution for your image. A higher image resolution does not always give superior printed results. In fact, an unnecessarily high image resolution increases the size of the file and causes a longer print time without improving the printed results (the printer discards the additional data that it cannot handle). On the other hand, a scan resolution that's too low degrades the quality of your output.

Image resolution (ppi)

30 ppi   300 ppi

Image resolution represents the number of pixels in a given measurement and is measured in pixels per inch (ppi). A high image resolution contains enough data to show more detail in the image, both on screen and in print; a very low-resolution image can appear jagged.

Halftone frequency (lpi)

60 lpi   150 lpi

Halftone frequency, also known as screen frequency or screen ruling, determines the size for the halftone cells (which are made of printer dots) that make up a printed image and is measured in lines per inch (lpi). The relationship between the dpi and the lpi influences how fine or coarse an image appears on the printed output.

Printer resolution (dpi)

Low printer resolution   High printer resolution

Most imagesetter and printer output consists of dots. Printer output resolution is measured in dots per inch (dpi). The higher the printer resolution, the better the appearance of the halftone cells.

Determining image resolution for printed media

To figure the ideal grayscale or true-color image resolution for printed media, you need to know the halftone frequency used by the output device. If you are printing on a local printer, check the printer's documentation. If the image is to be printed commercially, ask your service provider what halftone frequency to use.

Since there isn't a one-to-one correspondence between pixels and printer dots, you need to estimate how many pixels of information a printer or imagesetter can represent. Multiplying the halftone frequency by 2 is a conservative approach but may result in scanning at too high a resolution. In some cases multiplying the halftone frequency by as little as 1.5 still yields good results.

Scanning line art

In line art images, pixels are either black or white, so the biggest concern is having enough pixels to smoothly define the detail in your image. As a general rule, scan line art at the resolution of the output device or the highest scanner resolution. Keep in mind, however, that scanning at high resolutions creates large image files.

$$\frac{\text{final image height}}{\text{original image height}} \; \textbf{X} \; \text{halftone frequency} \; \textbf{X} \; 2 \; = \; \text{desired image resolution}$$

Example: Printing on a desktop laser printer

You want to scan an image 4 inches wide by 5 inches tall for a small newsletter that will be output to a desktop laser printer. In the newsletter, you have a 3-by-3.75-inch space for a grayscale image. The default halftone frequency for your printer is 60 lpi.

1. Calculate the ideal image resolution for scanning:
   (3.75 / 5) x 60 x 2 = 90 ppi.
2. Set the scanner resolution to 90 ppi and scan the image.

Example: Printing on a high resolution printer

You want to scan a 2-by-3-inch image to send to a commercial service provider for imaging and printing at the image's original size. The service provider has told you that the image will be printed with a halftone frequency of 133 lpi.

1. Calculate the ideal image resolution for scanning (since the image will be printed at its original size, you do not need to include the scaling factor):
   133 x 2 = 266 ppi.
2. Set the scanner resolution to 266 ppi and scan the image.

Determining image resolution for film recorder output

Like image resolution, film recorder output is measured in pixels. Film recorder resolution is based on the largest dimension (height or width) of the image. This formula uses the relationship between the film recorder pixels and the image pixels to determine the appropriate image resolution.

$$\frac{\text{film recorder resolution}}{\text{greatest dimension of original image}} = \text{desired image resolution}$$

Example: Scanning an image for slide output

You want to reproduce a 4-by-5-inch color photo as a slide. Your film recorder has an output resolution of 4000 lines per inch.

1. Calculate the ideal scanning resolution: 4000 / 5 = 800 ppi.

2. Set the scanner resolution to 800 ppi and scan the image.

3. Keep in mind that scanning at a resolution this high can produce very large files. In this example, the resulting file size would be 37.5MB. Before scanning files of this size, ensure your computer has enough RAM and disk space to accommodate it.

Determining image resolution for video or screen output

Video resolution is measured in pixels. This formula finds the relationship between the viewable video pixels and the image pixels to determine the appropriate image resolution to display the image across the entire screen.

You can also use this formula to calculate image resolution for television (as opposed to computer) video output. The width of a video frame in NISC format, an American standard, is 5̶2̶5̶ ⁷⁵⁶ pixels. To determine your desired image resolution, divide 5̶2̶5̶ ₇₅₆ by the width of your source image.

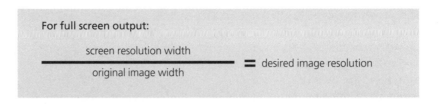

For full screen output:

$$\frac{\text{screen resolution width}}{\text{original image width}} = \text{desired image resolution}$$

Example: Scanning an image for full-screen output

You want to scan a 4-by-3-inch image for output to a computer screen. The screen is set to 640 by 480 pixels and you want the image to fill the entire screen.

1. Calculate the ideal image resolution for scanning:
   640 / 4 = 160 ppi.
2. Set the scanner resolution to 160 ppi and scan the image.

For actual-size output on screen:

$$\frac{\text{greatest dimension of screen resolution}}{\text{maximum displayable screen width}} = \text{desired image resolution}$$

Example: Scanning an image for actual-size screen output

You want to scan a 4-by-3-inch image for output to a computer screen and you want the image to appear on screen at its original size. The screen is set to 800 by 600 pixels and has a maximum displayable width of 11.75 inches (determined by measuring the screen with a ruler).

1. Calculate the ideal image resolution for scanning:
   800 / 11.75 = 68 ppi.
2. Set the scanner resolution to 68 ppi and scan the image.

Scanning an image

PhotoStyler provides links to the scanner driver, and the driver provides controls for the scanner. The options that appear under the Scan submenu on the File menu depend on the scanner driver you've chosen. Please consult your scanner documentation for information about these options and instructions for operating your scanner.

Tips for producing the best possible scan

Plan ahead. To produce the best-quality scan for your output, you need to know the final output device, the output requirements, and the final dimensions of your image.

Clean the glass. Remove dust or any other grit that would appear as a speck in your scanned image.

Use high-quality artwork. When working with photorealistic images, you'll get the best results from scanning an original, continuous-tone image.

$$\frac{\text{image}}{\text{height}} \; \mathbf{X} \; \frac{\text{image}}{\text{width}} \; \mathbf{X} \; \left(\frac{\text{scan}}{\text{resolution}} \right)^2 \; \mathbf{X} \; \frac{\text{bytes per}}{\text{pixel}} \; \mathbf{=} \; \frac{\text{approximate}}{\text{file size}}$$

Image type	Bytes per pixel
Black and white	0.125
Indexed 16-color	0.5
Indexed 256-color	1
Grayscale	1
RGB true color	3
CMYK true color	4

To scan an image

1. To scan an image from within PhotoStyler, you need either a TWAIN data source or a proprietary driver from your scanner manufacturer. If you don't have the correct driver, contact the scanner manufacturer.

2. Once the driver is installed, and you are ready to scan, choose Select Scanner... from the Scan submenu on the File menu to select the scanner you wish to use with PhotoStyler.

3. If you find that you apply the same commands from the Tune submenu on the Image menu to each scan, you can invoke up to six of these commands automatically after each scan. To do this, check Post Process and select the desired commands from the list boxes. Then click OK.

4. Choose Acquire... or Start Scan... from the Scan submenu on the File menu (the wording of the command varies depending on the installed scanner driver).

5. Before you start the scan, you should note the file size of the resulting image to make sure you have adequate hard disk space. Most scanner software interfaces show the file size. If your software does not show the file size, use the formula above.

Correcting common scanning problems

My scanned image is too dark.

Try using the scanner's interface to brighten the image by 5 or 10 percent. If this does not work, use the Tonal Correction... command on the Tune submenu on the Image menu to increase the image gamma.

My scanned image is too big or too small (width and height).

If the scanning software has a scaling option, adjust it and rescan the image. Or, use the Resample... command on the Image menu to resize the image.

My scanned image is crooked.

If possible, rescan the image to ensure it is straight. Or use the Level Horizontal or Level Vertical command on the Rotate submenu on the Image menu to straighten the image.

My scanned image is blurry.

Ensure the original image is the best possible quality and the scanner glass is clean. Or use the Focus... command on the Tune submenu on the Image menu to sharpen the image.

My scanned image is upside down or backwards.

If possible, rescan the image in the proper orientation. Or use one of the commands on the Flip submenu on the Image menu.

My scanned image is speckled.

Ensure the original image is the best possible quality and the scanner glass is clean and rescan the image. If this does not correct the problem, use the Despeckle... command on the Noise submenu on the Effects menu.

I had to scan a halftone (printed) image and the scanned image has moiré patterns.

Whenever possible, scan the original artwork. If you have only a halftone (printed) image, scan it at twice the required resolution, and then use the Resample... command on the Image menu to bring the resolution down to the correct level. If there is still some moiré, use the Blur... or Average... command on the Soften submenu on the Effects menu to lessen the moiré pattern.

Changing the size and resolution of an image

Use the Resample... and Resolution... commands on the Image menu to change the size and/or resolution of an image.

- Use the Resample... command when you need to convert the active image to a specific size (height and width) and resolution. Resample... changes the entire image; to change the size of a selection area within an image, choose a command from the Resize submenu on the Image menu.
- Use the Resolution... command if you want to define a new resolution only (without regard to the image dimensions). Resolution... by itself does not change the image file size (in bytes).

Resample...

The Resample... command lets you change the resolution and the dimensions of an image.

When you increase the dimensions of an image without decreasing the resolution, resampling compares the information in neighboring pixels and adds new pixels that maintain smooth transitions. This process is called interpolation. For better results, you may want to rescan the image with a higher scale factor.

When you decrease the dimensions of an image without increasing the resolution, resampling averages the pixel information to determine which pixels to remove.

If you're working with a photorealistic image, you may sacrifice some image detail when pixels are added or removed from the image. In many cases, the commands on the Sharpen submenu on the Effects menu can help you regain the sharpness of your image (although they cannot replace data that was lost during resampling).

Since Resample... adds or removes pixels as needed, the image file size (in bytes) may change.

Resolution...

The Resolution... command lets you change the defined resolution of an image without adding or deleting pixels. It does, however, change the image dimensions. For example, suppose you have an image that has a resolution of 300 pixels per inch (ppi). If you use the Resolution...

command to set the resolution to 100 ppi, you have not changed the number of pixels in the image; rather, you have redefined how many pixels there are in each inch. Therefore, the height and width of the 100 ppi image are each three times greater than the height and width of the 300 ppi version.

Because the Resolution... command does not change the total number of pixels in the image, it cannot increase the sharpness or level of detail of an image.

Example: Resampling to adjust the image resolution

You have a color image that is the correct height and width, and the image resolution is 300 ppi. Your prepress service provider tells you that the halftone frequency you need is 133 lpi. You want to reduce the image resolution to 266 ppi (133 x 2; see page 55 for more information) to avoid unnecessary output time on the imagesetter.

1. Choose Resample… from the Image menu.
2. For Resolution, type in 266 ppi.
3. Check Create New Document to resample the existing image and create a new one with the resolution you specified.
4. For Lock, select Print Size to keep the output size the same. Then click OK.

Note: The new image appears smaller on screen because it has fewer pixels to display, but it will print at the correct size. You can verify the dimensions by choosing Image Information… from the View menu.

Example: Resampling to adjust the image dimensions and resolution

You have an 8-by-10-inch image with a resolution of 300 ppi. You need a 4-by-5-inch image to use in an on-screen presentation. The output screen is set to 640 by 480 pixels, so you need a resolution of 128 ppi (640 / 5; see page 57 for more information).

1. Choose Resample… from the Image menu.
2. For New Image Information, select inches from the top list box and type in 4 for height and 5 for width.
3. For Resolution, type in 128.
4. Check Create New Document to resample the existing image and create a new one with your specifications.
5. For Lock, select None and click OK.

Example: Changing image resolution to adjust image size

You scan in a 4-by-5-inch image at a resolution of 90 ppi. You later learn that the image must be 3 by 3.75 inches and that the halftone frequency is 60 lpi. To find the new resolution, multiply the current resolution by the ratio of the current and desired image sizes (90 x 5 / 3.75 = 120). Notice that the new resolution of 120 is also appropriate for a halftone frequency of 60 lpi (60 x 2).

1. Choose Resolution… from the Image menu.
2. Select User-Defined and type in 120.
3. Click OK.

Resampling as you crop

The cropping tool lets you resample the image while cropping; this is very useful if you are preparing an image to fit in a predefined spot in a page layout publication, such as Aldus PageMaker. This performs the same function as if you cropped and then used the Resample… command on the Image menu. The advantage is that it's all done in a single step and can save you a lot of time if you have numerous images to prepare.

To crop and resample simultaneously

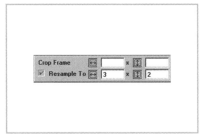
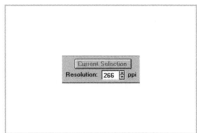

1. Select the cropping tool from the Tools palette.

2. Type in the dimensions of the desired final image in the Resample To width and height boxes on the tool ribbon.

3. Type in the resolution of the final image in Resolution (ppi).

4. Drag the cropping frame around the portion of the image you wish to use. The cropping frame is constrained to the height-width ratio you specified.

5. Click Crop on the tool ribbon or double-click anywhere inside the cropping frame.

6. Save the image to place into your publication.

Printing and
Other Output

Getting a PhotoStyler image to final output

Once you have enhanced a PhotoStyler image, you can prepare it to be included in printed material, in presentations using slides or transparencies, or in on-screen presentations, multimedia, or video applications.

Advances in desktop printing technology continue to narrow the gap between high-end commercial printing and desktop printing. Your final output may be printed using any one of these printing devices:

- Black-and-white desktop printers, such as the Hewlett-Packard LaserJet series or PostScript printers
- High-resolution desktop printers, such as the LaserMaster series
- Color composite printers, such as the QMS ColorScript 100 printer and the Kodak XL 7700 and 7720
- High-resolution imagesetters, such as the Linotronic, AGFA Select Set, and AGFA Pro Set series

You may work with one or more service providers: a slide service bureau, a prepress service bureau, or a commercial print shop.

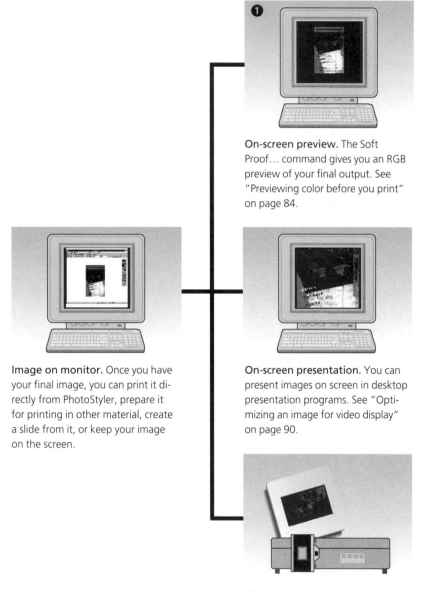

On-screen preview. The Soft Proof… command gives you an RGB preview of your final output. See "Previewing color before you print" on page 84.

Image on monitor. Once you have your final image, you can print it directly from PhotoStyler, prepare it for printing in other material, create a slide from it, or keep your image on the screen.

On-screen presentation. You can present images on screen in desktop presentation programs. See "Optimizing an image for video display" on page 90.

Film recorder. To create 35mm slides, print your image on a slide film recorder or send it to a slide service bureau. See "Printing on a film recorder" on page 92.

Select a Precision Transform for your final output type or device. To ensure accurate color, you must use the KODAK PRECISION Color Management System to target your project to your final printing or proofing method. See "Selecting a Precision Transform for final output" on page 80.

Convert to CMYK and place in another application. If your image will be printed from separations as part of a desktop-published document, your next step may be to convert the image into CMYK format. See "Object linking and embedding (OLE)" on page 72 and "Tips for placing an image in another application" on page 74.

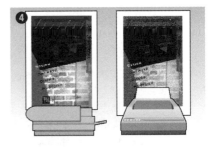

Low-resolution proofs. Printing on a black-and-white or color desktop printer gives you a rough proof for overall design. Though limited by low resolution and color quality, under some circumstances output from these printers can also be final output. See "Printing on a monochrome printer" on page 87 and "Working with proofing and final printers" on page 82.

Color separations. You can print paper or film separations directly from PhotoStyler or have a service provider print them. See "Printing color separations" on page 88.

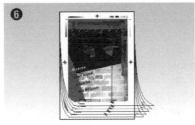

Industry-standard proofs. Next to a press check, separation-based color proofs are the most accurate proofs available. Overlay proofs or laminated proofs can provide reliable methods for color forecasting and identifying potential problems, but can be expensive. See "Color proofs" on page 85.

Commercial printer. If you are creating high-resolution black-and-white material, a service provider typically creates film from your camera-ready paper output or your files on disk and prints the final output. If you are creating high-resolution color material, a print shop runs the plates on a dedicated printing press. See "Working with service providers" on page 71.

Printing terminology

Continuous-tone art

If you look closely at an original black-and-white or color photograph, you'll see that the image consists of solid shades of gray or color that blend smoothly. An original photograph is called continuous-tone art.

Strictly speaking, commercial printing processes can't reproduce the continuous tones of a photograph. However, commercial printers approach the effect of continuous tones by using black ink for black-and-white photographs and grayscale images and by blending process inks (cyan, magenta, yellow, and black) for color photographs. Dye sublimation printers, such as the Kodak XL 7700 and 7720 and the Tektronix II SD, blend dyes instead of ink to give the effect of continuous tones.

Halftone screens

To reproduce continuous-tone art on a commercial printing press, the image must be broken into a series of dots, called a halftone screen. In photographic halftoning, halftone dots can vary infinitely in size to indicate light and dark areas. In digital halftoning, halftone dots must be the same size. To indicate light and dark areas, halftone dots are combined into cells; a greater density of dots per cell indicates a dark area, while a smaller number of dots indicates a lighter area. The more dots a halftone cell contains, the more possible gray levels it can represent.

Screen frequency, or halftone frequency, is the spacing of halftone cells per inch (also called line screen or line frequency because the cells are aligned in rows) and is measured in lines per inch (lpi). A higher screen frequency means more halftone cells per inch.

Screen angle, or halftone angle, defines the orientation of the line of halftone cells. For black-and-white images, the screen angle is generally 45 degrees. For CMYK color printing, screen angles are: black, 45 degrees; magenta, 75 degrees; yellow, 90 degrees; and cyan, 105 degrees.

Dot shape specifies the shape of the half-tone cells. Cells are usually round, but they can also be elliptical, square, or other shapes for specific image types or for special effects.

Dot gain

Dot gain occurs when ink is absorbed into paper and creates larger halftone dots than intended. The more absorbent the paper, or the thinner the ink, the greater the dot gain. If you are printing your work commercially, your service provider can tell you what settings to use for dot gain compensation. For more information, see "Setting halftone and dot gain options" on page 79.

Halftone dots in a color proof

The same image after printing

Paper types

The paper you select for a particular project has a significant impact on the quality of your final output. The weight and absorbency of the paper are two important factors in the selection of paper stock. If you want professional-quality reproduction, you need to match it with paper that can accept the required higher screen frequency. If you are printing on newsprint, you know from the start that you can use a lower frequency.

Screen frequency is inversely related to paper absorbency. For newsprint, which is quite absorbent, a frequency of 85 lpi or less is standard; for uncoated paper stock, 120 lpi or less; and for coated paper stock, up to 300 lpi. Whenever you are printing at screen frequencies of 100 lpi or higher, outputting separations directly to film instead of to paper avoids dot gain at the separations step.

Printer resolution

Printer resolution specifies the number of dots that print per inch. This number, divided by the screen frequency, determines how many dots are used in each halftone cell. The more dots that are used, the more shades of gray are available. However, at a given printer resolution, there is a tradeoff between the number of gray levels and the screen frequency. For more information on resolution, see "What is resolution?" on page 54.

Process colors

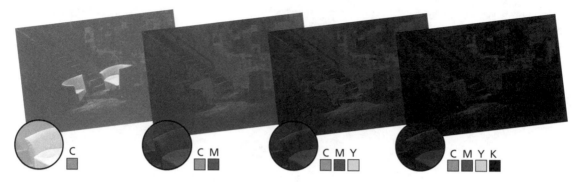

Color images are reproduced on paper using process colors. Process colors are created by printing overlapping dots (halftone screens) of cyan, magenta, and yellow (CMY) inks to simulate a large number of different colors. To create blue, for example, cyan dots (which absorb red and reflect blue and green) and magenta dots (which absorb green and reflect blue and red) are combined. Your eyes merge the cyan and magenta to perceive the color blue. The four process colors create the largest number of colors using the least number of printing inks.

You could, in theory, mix 100% of cyan, magenta, and yellow to create black. However, you never print 100% of these inks for two reasons: (1) Inks are imperfect, and printing this combination of cyan, magenta, and yellow creates a muddy brown color instead of a sharp black. (2) Printing too much ink on a particular area of a page oversaturates that area, causing the quality of the printing to deteriorate. To achieve fine detail and strong shadows in print, printers use black ink (K) along with cyan, magenta, and yellow inks (CMYK).

Gamut

Every device has a range of colors that it can produce, called a gamut. In addition, every image has a range of colors that makes up that image on the screen. Out-of-gamut images contain colors that the printer or output device can't produce. The color management system ensures that the image you see on your screen is exactly what is printed— you do not see any colors that are out of the printer's gamut. For more information, see "The KODAK PRECISION Color Management System" on page 9.

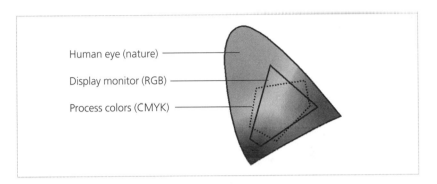

Human eye (nature)

Display monitor (RGB)

Process colors (CMYK)

Separations

To print professional-quality images on a commercial printing press, you first separate the page containing the composite art into its component colors by printing a separation for each ink—cyan, magenta, yellow, and black—needed to print the colors in the image. Your printer uses these separations to create the printing plates used on the press.

File storage and transfer

Some of your PhotoStyler image files may be quite large—30MB or more. If you are used to delivering your files to a service provider on disk, or if you need to transfer your files to another computer without a network, you may wonder how you'll move these large files.

There are two common methods for transferring large files: external storage devices and modems.

To save additional space on a removable hard drive or to decrease the size of files you send by modem, you may want to compress your image files. Be sure to use a compression format that the service bureau can decompress. Because the JPEG format is "lossy"—that is, image information is lost during compression—you may not want to use JPEG compression for some files. Although it does not result in file sizes as small as those from JPEG compression, LZW compression retains all image information.

External storage devices

Using an external storage device, such as a Bernouilli or Syquest removable hard drive, you can create a print file and then give the hard drive to your imagesetter or service provider.

Storage space is like memory: you can never have too much. Plan for extra space on your external storage device.

Be sure to ask your service provider how they transfer large files. Some service providers aren't set up to work with PC-based storage devices.

Modems

Modems let you send image data over phone lines to your imagesetter or to other members of a work-group. The transmission speed for data sent across telecommunications networks is measured in bits per second.

If you plan to send image files directly to a service provider, be sure to ask what settings you need so your modems work together.

If you're used to sending text-only files by modem, you may notice that it takes significantly longer to send image data.

Working with service providers

If you work regularly with commercial-quality images, you may also work with several service providers. Service providers—slide service bureaus, prepress service bureaus, and commercial printers—help you get your image to the final output you want. Select your service providers as soon as you start a project and communicate with them throughout the project.

If your final output is printed material, you will probably work most closely with a prepress service bureau, or color house, and a commercial printer, or print shop. Because prepress and printing processes are closely related, find a service bureau and printer who work well with you and with each other.

When you start discussions with service providers about a project, explain your layout and page setup, if appropriate, and the budget and time constraints you are working within. You will also want their advice on press control options, such as halftone shape, screen angle, and frequency.

Questions for a commercial printer

- For film output, do they want the film emulsion up or down? Right-reading or wrong-reading?
- Have they worked with images produced on the desktop?
- Do they have recommendations for paper stock (weight, color, texture)?
- Do they have recommendations for inks?
- What settings do they recommend for screen angle, screen frequency, and halftone shape based on your paper and ink selections?
- What proofing method or methods do they offer? Which do they recommend for your project?
- Will dot gain be compensated for in advance (through PhotoStyler settings) or during prepress work?

Questions for a prepress service bureau

- Are they familiar with PhotoStyler or other image-editing programs?
- Do they accept PC-based media? If not, how do they transfer large files?
- What software do they have on the PC or on the Macintosh? This is helpful to know in case additional work needs to be done on your files.

- What requirements do they have for preparing files for output? Are they willing to work with you to develop your hand-off instructions? Do they charge for this time?
- What file formats and data types can they work with?
- Do they require a preseparated file, RGB file, or print-to-disk file?
- What compression do they recommend for files they receive?
- Will they advise you on screen frequency, screen angle, and halftone shape settings, or will they set these? Are they working with the printer to determine the best settings for your chosen paper and inks?
- What printing equipment do they use? Different printers have different resolution and different limitations.
- Will you receive proofs from the service bureau? What proof options do they offer?

Object linking and embedding (OLE)

PhotoStyler supports the Windows Object Linking and Embedding (OLE) 1.0 specification for sharing data between Windows applications. OLE extends the familiar Paste command found in most Windows programs by letting you create an active link between the program that creates the object and the program into which you paste the object. For example, you can use OLE to link PhotoStyler image files to an Aldus PageMaker publication so the images in the publication are updated whenever the original images are modified.

Since PhotoStyler creates the image object, it is referred to as the *source*, and the program into which you paste is called the *destination*.

OLE provides two ways to include and update PhotoStyler images in a destination file: you can link the image so the image file remains separate from the destination file, or you can embed the image so it becomes a part of the destination file. You can OLE-link or OLE-embed an entire PhotoStyler image or a portion of the image that you have copied to the Windows Clipboard.

Linking

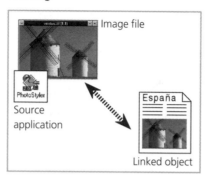

Linked object

When you link a PhotoStyler image to a destination application, the image file does not become a part of the destination application's file. Instead, the destination application file stores the directory and filename of the image. The linked object updates automatically when the original image is modified, as long as the original image is linked to the destination file. The PhotoStyler image must be saved to create an OLE link.

Linking is advantageous when you need to use an image repeatedly. This lets you update all instances of the image object—even in multiple destination files—by editing the original and updating the links. Since the image object is saved only once, linking a single image to multiple destinations saves more disk space than embedding. If you copy the destination application file to another computer, it is necessary to also copy all the linked image files.

Embedding

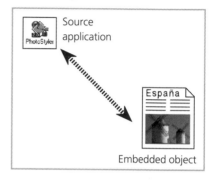

Embedded object

When you embed a PhotoStyler image in a destination file, the image becomes a part of that file. Because of this, the image does not need to be saved to its own file. Embedding is appropriate when you have only one copy of an image in the destination file. The advantage is that all the information you need to edit the image is within the destination file, so you don't have to keep track of an original image. However, doing so increases the size of the destination file, taking up more disk space. Furthermore, if the same image is embedded in more than one place, each embedded image must be edited separately. In this case, it is probably better to use linking.

To embed or link an existing image in a destination file

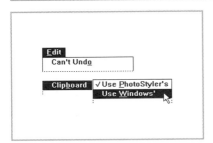  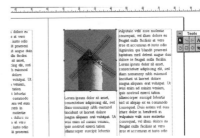

1. Start PhotoStyler and open the image.

2. Choose Use Windows' from the Clipboard submenu on the Edit menu.

3. Select the area of the image you want to copy. If you want to select the entire image, press Ctrl + A or click the select all button on the Tools palette.

4. Copy the selection to the Windows Clipboard by pressing Ctrl + C.

5. Switch to the destination application. Paste the contents of the Clipboard as specified in the application's documentation.

To edit an embedded or linked image

1. Consult the destination application's documentation for the exact procedure for editing OLE objects. For many applications, you double-click the image in the destination application and OLE will open the image in PhotoStyler.

2. Once PhotoStyler starts and the image is loaded, you can edit the image.

3. When you are done editing the image, choose Update <destination application name> from the File menu and switch back to the destination application.

Tips for placing an image in another application

After you have retouched an image in PhotoStyler, you may place your color or grayscale image in another application and print it from there.

Before placing images

If you plan to make color separations for commercial reproduction, you often convert your image to a CMYK TIFF image before placing it in another application.

When you place a CMYK TIFF in your document, it's critical that it is all targeted to the correct device. For example, if you target an image to a low-resolution printer and convert the image to CMYK, the gamut of the image is mapped to the low-resolution device. If you then place the image in a page-layout program and decide to print at high resolution, the image won't reflect the optimized gamut for that device. To use the optimized gamut, return to the original RGB image in PhotoStyler and designate your proofing method, like Matchprint, or your final output device before converting the image to CMYK. For more information, see "Selecting a Precision Transform for final output" on page 80.

If you've compressed your image, remember that you may need to decompress it before your page-layout program can recognize it. If you use JPEG compression, you will lose some image data; the higher the compression, the greater the data loss.

Be sure the image is cropped to the correct size and at the correct resolution before you place it in another application.

If you want to rotate an image, use the commands on the Rotate submenu on the Image menu to rotate the image before placing it in a page-layout program. Objects rotated in page-layout programs take longer to print.

Copying using the Windows Clipboard

You can use the Windows Clipboard to copy an image to another Windows application. However, the Windows Clipboard is not optimized for the size and quality of images in PhotoStyler. If you use the Windows Clipboard, it may not be able to support all image information and your image may lose quality.

Working with images during production and proofing

To speed production work and create an initial proof of a publication that includes images, you may want to duplicate your final images and resample them at a lower resolution to speed printing. You can also print images at a low screen frequency during layout and proofing phases. Be sure to increase the screen frequency at final output stage.

If you want to tile an image while printing, you can do it within PhotoStyler by selecting the Tile option in the Print dialog box. If you want to customize the tile size, import the image into an application that supports custom tiling, such as Aldus PageMaker or Aldus FreeHand.

Selecting printing options

Three PhotoStyler commands on the Print submenu of the File menu— Print..., Options..., and Printer Setup...—let you set printing options. Choosing Print... lets you select options such as printing printers' marks and printing an image as a negative. Choosing Options... from the Print submenu or from the Print dialog box gives you additional printing options, such as screen frequency, screen angle, and halftone settings. Settings in the Print and Options dialog boxes are covered in the next four pages.

Before you print from PhotoStyler, you must install and configure a Windows-compatible printer driver for your printer. If you are proofing your image or publication on one printer but intend to print the final version on another printer, you need to install both printers in Windows and select the Precision Transform for the final output device from the KODAK PRECISION Color Management System (CMS).

Some settings, such as those for halftones, separations, and calibration, are available from both PhotoStyler and the printer driver. Selecting By PhotoStyler in the appropriate section of the Options dialog box overrides the printer driver settings and gives PhotoStyler control over these settings. Selecting

By Printer gives you partial control over the settings. Some options remain available; those that are dimmed are controlled by the printer driver. Selecting By Printer and Use Printer's Defaults lets the Windows printer driver control the printing settings. If you are using another printer driver, selecting By Printer and Use Printer's Defaults lets you use the options provided by that driver as well.

The Halftone section of the Options dialog box lets you set options for screen angle, screen frequency, and dot shape. The Separations section of the Options dialog box lets you set options for dot gain. The Calibration section lets you set the output range and use a custom gamma curve.

Choosing a page orientation setting in PhotoStyler always overrides the printer driver setting, even if you have selected By Printer and Use Printer's Defaults.

Printing dialog boxes

Print dialog box overview

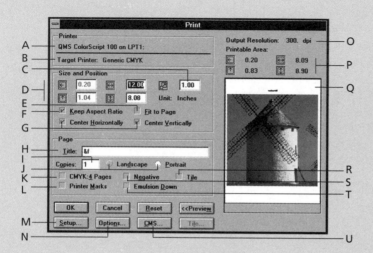

A Name and port of the current Windows-selected printer.

B Name of the selected Precision Transform, which assigns the characteristics of the final output device to images.

C Lets you scale an image before printing by typing the reduction or enlargement from the default, 1.00.

D For the active image, lets you type in the size and position from the upper left corner of the page, using the current measurement unit.

E Scales the image to fit on the page.

F Preserves the image proportions when the size of the image or the printed area changes.

G Centers the image on the page horizontally or vertically.

H Lets you enter text to appear above the image. The default, &f, prints the image title. Adding &t prints the date and time. Clearing the text box means that no text is printed with the image file.

I Lets you type in the number of copies you want to print.

J Lets you select whether the page prints portrait or landscape.

K Prints four separation pages, one for each CMYK color.

L Prints crop marks, registration marks, a calibration bar, and a color bar on the page.

M Opens the Windows Setup dialog box to choose or view the current printer.

N Opens the Options dialog box.

O Shows the resolution of the selected printer.

P On the left, shows the size of the page margins; on the right, shows the dimensions of the page that can be used for printing.

Q Shows a low-resolution version of the image in the image area you have defined. Shows tiles when Tile is checked.

R When the image size exceeds the page size, the Tile check box and the Tile… button become available. Click Tile… to set the amount of overlap between tiles. PhotoStyler does not let you customize tile size.

S Prints film or paper separations as negatives. Leave unchecked to print as positives.

T Lets you choose whether to print with the emulsion up or down. Ask your service provider for the proper setting.

U Lets you view or change the Precision Transform of the final output device.

Options dialog box overview

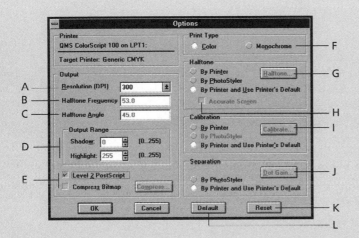

H Check if you are printing to a PostScript Level 2 device and want to use Adobe's improved screen angle technology. Using Accurate Screen reduces moirés in your PostScript output.

I Opens the Printer Calibration dialog box. For more information on calibration settings, see "Selecting printing options" on page 75.

J Opens the Dot Gain dialog box. For more information on separation settings, see "Selecting printing options" on page 75 and "Setting halftone and dot gain options" on page 79.

K Resets values to last-saved settings.

L Sets all options to defaults.

A Shows the resolution of the selected printer and lets you select from available printer resolution options.

B Lets you change the current halftone frequency.

C Lets you change the screen angle for black-and-white printing. Use the default (45 degrees) unless you want special effects.

D Lets you control highlight and shadow cut-off points. For more information, see "Setting output range" on page 78.

E When printing PostScript Level 2, checking this option compresses bitmaps to create a smaller file at print. Click Compress... to specify JPEG or LZW compression.

F Select Monochrome if you are printing to a black-and-white printer. Select Color if you are printing to a color composite printer.

G Specify dot shape, screen frequency, and screen angle for halftone images or color separations. For more information on halftone settings, see "Selecting printing options" on page 75 and "Setting halftone and dot gain options" on page 79.

Setting output range

The range of gray or color values in an original digital image is called the input range. Adjusting the image during image correction or printing changes the range of values. This is called the output range. Many of the commands on the Tune submenu on the Image menu change the output range of an image.

You may want to change the range of gray or color values in an image at the time you print. The Output Range section of the Options dialog box lets you control highlight and shadow cut-off points, where 0 corresponds to black and 255 corresponds to white. To increase the shadow cut-off point, increase the number in the Shadow text box from 0; to reduce the highlight cut-off point, decrease the number in the Highlight text box from 255.

If you select By Printer and Use Printer's Defaults, the selected printer determines the output range of the image and the Output Range section in the Options dialog box is unavailable.

Gray or color values on the 0 to 255 scale are accurate in defining output range. However, your service provider may recommend an output range in percentage. Use the Percentage to gray value conversion table to determine the correct numbers to enter in the Output Range section of the Options dialog box. For example, your service provider may ask you to increase shadows and decrease highlights by 5%. In this case, you type 13 (an increase of 13) in the Shadow text box and 242 (a decrease of 13) in the Highlight text box.

Percentage to gray value conversion table

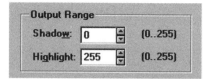

Percentage	Gray value
0%	0
5%	13
10%	26
15%	38
20%	51
25%	64
30%	77
35%	89
40%	102
45%	115
50%	128
55%	140
60%	153
65%	166
70%	179
75%	191
80%	204
85%	217
90%	230
95%	242
100%	255

Setting halftone and dot gain options

The color management system (CMS) has predetermined halftone and dot gain settings for your selected final output device. Under most conditions, you do not need to adjust these settings. You may, however, change halftone dot shape if you want a shape other than the default round shape.

If you want to adjust other halftone settings, you should select a different Precision Transform by double-clicking the Color Configure icon in the Windows Control Panel. For more information, see "The KODAK PRECISION Color Management System" on page 9

In some cases, a commercial printer may direct you to compensate for dot gain. Changing dot gain settings can have a drastic effect on your printed output. Change them only if you are absolutely certain that it is required.

To specify halftone dot shape

1. Choose Options… from the Print submenu on the File menu or click Options… in the Print dialog box.
2. In the Halftone section, select By PhotoStyler. Then click Halftone….
3. Select a halftone dot shape from the drop-down list box.
4. Click OK. Click OK again to close the Options dialog box. The default halftone shape is now the shape you selected. If you want to return to the round halftone dot shape for other images, select Round again.

Elliptical dots produce a softer printed image, which can be appropriate for a portrait. Diamond dots increase contrast and are suitable for landscape images. Square dots are best for reproducing shadows and highlights but not midtones, while round dots are best for reproducing midtones. Other dot shapes are useful for creating special effects.

To compensate for dot gain

1. Choose Options… from the Print submenu on the File menu.
2. In the Separation section, select By PhotoStyler. Then click Dot Gain….
3. To adjust all ink levels by the same amount, choose By Percent and type in a value.
4. Click OK to accept the new value. Click OK again to close the Options dialog box.

It is important to remember that the numbers you enter in By Percent indicate the reduction in dot gain. For example, your printer may tell you that they want 80% ink coverage overall to compensate for dot gain on press. In the Dot Gain dialog box, you enter 20 in the By Percent box. This reduces the dot gain by 20%, giving you 80% ink coverage. You can also reduce dot gain by individual channels by selecting By Measurement and typing in the desired values. This is a highly specialized function and not one you're likely to need for most printing jobs.

Selecting a Precision Transform for final output

You must specify the Precision Transform (PT) before you convert an image to CMYK. Through the PT, the color management system (CMS) assigns the attributes of the selected output type to the image.

You can specify a PT through the CMS when you install PhotoStyler, in the Open Image File, Save Image File, or Print dialog boxes, or when you convert an image to CMYK. If you do not specify a PT, you will be unable to convert the image to CMYK.

You can select final output devices, such as black-and-white and color printers and web offset presses, or you can select output types, such as Cromalin and Matchprint proofs. You and your service providers should decide which PT best suits the needs of your project before you select a PT.

Don't confuse the final output type or PT with the Windows printer driver. If your ultimate output type is a Matchprint or a commercial printing press, specify the PT for that proofing method or press type. In addition, if you want to print an image file directly, you need the correct Windows printer driver to do so. For more information, see "Printing an image to disk" on page 86.

When you convert an RGB image to CMYK, the CMS uses the selected PT to create a CMYK image. The image you see on the screen does not contain any colors that are outside the range of colors, or gamut, of the final output device or industry-standard proof type you selected in the PT.

If you want to change the final output device or proof type, you must do so before you convert an RGB image to CMYK. Once an image is converted to CMYK, you cannot apply a new PT to it. Do not attempt to convert the image back to RGB and then to CMYK to change the PT. Doing so will result in a loss of color data and image quality. Therefore, if you are working with an original RGB image, you should save a backup copy of the RGB version in case you want to use it with a different output type later on.

Tip: When converting an RGB image to CMYK, make sure New Image is checked on the Convert To submenu on the Image menu. This ensures that your original RGB image is preserved as a backup.

Even if you do not intend to print your final output directly from PhotoStyler (for example, if you are going to place the image in a page-layout program such as Aldus PageMaker), you must still specify the final output type for your CMYK images.

For more information about the color management system and Precision Transforms, see "The KODAK PRECISION Color Management System" on page 9.

To designate a Precision Transform for a final output type

1. When you are ready to convert your image to CMYK, choose CMYK from the Convert To submenu on the Image menu.

2. The CMS prompts you to select your final output type in the Select Output Device dialog box. Select a PT from the Output Device drop-down list. The space below the list provides information on the selected PT. If you don't find the PT you want in the drop-down list, use the following procedure to set up a new PT or use the default. When you are satisfied with your selection, click OK.

3. Choose Print… from the Print submenu on the File menu. Check that the name next to Target Printer in the upper left corner of the Print dialog box is the PT you selected. Click Cancel. You can now save the file and print it or print to disk.

To set up a new Precision Transform

1. If you do not find the PT you want in the Select Output Device dialog box, click the Color Configure… button.

2. In the Color Configure dialog box, click the Output button to view all the available PTs.

3. Click View to read information about the selected PT. This information can help you if you want specific settings, such as specific UCR and GCR percentages.

4. Select the output device or type that you want and click Select. If the PT you want is unavailable in the Color Configure dialog box, you can use the default PT for standard output on a wide range of devices.

5. Double-click the control menu box to close the Color Configure dialog box. The CMS will ask if you want to save the new setting. Click Yes to confirm.

To select a new input device or monitor, repeat this procedure using the Input and Monitor buttons in the Color Configure dialog box.

PhotoStyler Special Edition and the Kodak CMS

This special edition of PhotoStyler installs a default CMS configuration, but does not supply any additional PTs. Although the default configuration will produce good results, you may want to obtain the proper PTs if color accuracy is critical to your work. To find out about the availability of PTs for your system, contact Kodak at (800) 752-6567.

Working with proofing and final printers

As you work with PhotoStyler images, you are likely to encounter these three printing scenarios:

- Printing a final version directly from PhotoStyler through a selected Windows printer driver or third-party printer driver
- Printing a proof version on the current printer and then changing the selected printer to the final printer for the final version
- Printing a proof version on the current printer and handing off the image files for printing on a final output device elsewhere

Each scenario follows a slightly different procedure, given on the next page.

You specify the *final output type* for your PhotoStyler image when you select a Precision Transform (PT) through the KODAK PRECISION Color Management System (CMS). The printer that you have currently chosen in PhotoStyler (and Windows) is the selected printer or *current printer*. The CMS assigns the appropriate final output type attributes to the image, regardless of what is selected for the current printer.

If you haven't selected a PT for your final output type and you are printing CMYK images, see "Selecting a Precision Transform for final output" on page 80.

You can print both RGB and CMYK images from PhotoStyler. Some printers, such as the Kodak XL 7700 and 7720, take RGB data, though you can also print CMYK images to them. To print an RGB image, you still need to select the appropriate PT. If you are printing to a monochrome printer, convert your image to grayscale.

After you specify the final output type in the CMS (for CMYK images), you may use your current printer for proofing. The current printer prints your image using the PT of the final output type within the limits of the current printer's gamut. Once the image is ready, you can set the current printer to the same device as the final output device and print the final image if you have the correct driver.

To print on the current printer

You can select a current printer from those printers that have been added to the Windows Control Panel. For information on adding printers to Windows, see your Windows documentation.

1. Choose Printer Setup… from the Print submenu on the File menu. You should have the correct Windows printer driver installed. If you are printing a CMYK image, you should also have specified the correct final output type before converting the image to CMYK.

2. Select the final printer in the Printer Setup dialog box and click OK.

3. Choose Print… from the Print submenu on the File menu or press Ctrl + P.

4. Choose printing options in the appropriate printing dialog boxes.

5. Preview the way the image will print on the page in the Preview section of the Print dialog box. When you are satisfied with the print settings, click OK.

To print on the final printer

If you are making color separations or printing to a CMYK color printer, choose Soft Proof… from the File menu to preview your output. For more information, see "Previewing color before you print" on page 84.

1. For CMYK output, convert the image to CMYK, setting the output device when prompted. For more information, see "Selecting a Precision Transform for final output" on page 80. For grayscale output, convert the image to grayscale. See "Printing on a monochrome printer" on page 87.

2. Choose Printer Setup… from the Print submenu on the File menu.

3. Select the final printer in the Printer Setup dialog box and click OK.

4. Choose Print… from the Print submenu on the File menu or press Ctrl + P.

5. Choose printing options in the appropriate printing dialog boxes.

6. Preview the way the image will print on the page in the Preview section of the Print dialog box. When you are satisfied with the print settings, click OK.

To print on a remote final output device

Your final output device may not be on-site, as is typically the case when you hand off image files to a commercial printer. In this situation, you don't select the final output device in the Printer Setup dialog box.

1. If you are making color separations or printing to a CMYK color printer, convert the image to CMYK, setting the appropriate output device when prompted. For more information, see "Selecting a Precision Transform for final output" on page 80. For grayscale output, convert the image to grayscale. See "Printing on a monochrome printer" on page 87.

2. Prepare the image file for hand-off as requested by your service provider. For more information about printing separations, see "Printing color separations" on page 88.

Previewing color before you print

The color management system (CMS) ensures that the image displayed on your RGB screen matches the printed output. You can preview RGB and CMYK images before printing them using the Soft Proof... command on the File menu.

It is best to delay converting your image to CMYK until all editing is finished, because each conversion between RGB and CMYK color spaces results in loss of image information; multiple conversions cause the image to degenerate.

Use the Soft Proof... command to simulate on the monitor the way the image will appear in final output. Use Soft Proof... to simulate changing a Precision Transform or to preview an RGB image before converting it to CMYK. Soft Proof... displays the effect of RGB-to-CMYK conversion without affecting your image file and saves media and print time.

To preview an RGB image using Soft Proof...

1. Choose Soft Proof... from the File menu.

2. For an accurate preview, the correct final output device must be specified. To view or change the final output device, click the CMS... button. For more information on CMS , see "The KODAK PRECISION Color Management System" on page 9.

3. In the Soft Proof dialog box, specify whether you want your image displayed to fill the screen or in actual size. Then click OK.

4. If your final output is CMYK, the image displayed on screen is an RGB simulation of how the CMYK image will appear, based on the Precision Transform of the specified final output type. Click to zoom in, or press Shift and click to zoom out. No other tools are available while you are previewing the image.

5. When you are done reviewing the image, press Esc to return to the original RGB image.

Color proofs

Color proofing and printing used to be done only by high end commercial printers. In recent years, color desktop printers have greatly expanded the proofing and output capabilities available from the desktop. For most color images, final color proofing should still be done using separation-based, or industry-standard, proofs.

Desktop color printers come in a variety of quality levels, from 300 dpi color laser printers, such as QMS ColorScript 100 and Seiko Color Point, to high-resolution color printers, such as the Scitex Iris InkJet and the Kodak XL 7720. Color fidelity on low-resolution desktop printers may not be satisfactory.

Composite proofs can be printed on the desktop. For more information, see "Working with proofing and final printers" on page 82.

A service provider creates industry-standard proofs. If you want an industry-standard proof from your service provider, you should select the correct industry-standard proof type as your Precision Transform from the CMS. For more information, see "Selecting a Precision Transform for final output" on page 80.

Composite proofs

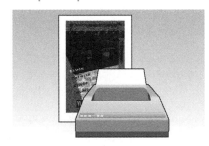

Color laser and continuous-tone printers. Color composite proofs are useful before you make color separations and an expensive printer's proof. Use a color composite proof to determine whether the file will print, to check image dimensions, and to review overall image detail. Do not use a color composite proof to check color accuracy or correction.

Continuous-tone color printer. High-quality proofs can be obtained from continuous-tone and dye-sublimation color desktop printers.

Industry-standard proofs

Overlay proof. Overlay proofs, such as 3M Color Key, are created by printing separations on acetate sheets colored to match the four process inks; the sheets are then layered on top of one another. Though economical, overlay proofs are less reliable than laminated proofs for checking final color.

Laminated proof. Laminated proofs, such as DuPont Cromalin and 3M Matchprint, are created by binding pigmented layers together into a single proof sheet. Laminated proofs are a reliable method for color forecasting and for identifying potential problems, such as moiré patterns.

Printing an image to disk

If your service provider doesn't own Aldus PhotoStyler, or if you simply want to ensure that your image settings remain unchanged, you can give your service provider a PostScript print file of your work. Making a print file is often called "printing to disk."

Don't worry if your file becomes larger when you print to disk. The print file is larger than your image file.

Once you create a PostScript file, you can copy it to a disk or to a removable hard disk or send it to a service bureau by modem.

If you are printing the final publication to disk for a service bureau, be sure the current printer selected matches the printer that the service bureau will use to print.

1. Start Windows Control Panel and double-click the Printers icon. Select the printer to which you will be sending your print file. If it isn't in the Installed Printers list, you will have to install it. For more information, refer to your Windows documentation.

2. Click Connect... and select FILE: from the Ports list. Then click OK. Close the Printers dialog box and exit Control Panel.

3. In PhotoStyler, choose Print... from the Print submenu on the File menu.

4. Click Setup... and select the printer you assigned to the FILE: port. Then click OK.

5. Adjust other print settings as desired and click OK.

Note: When you print to disk, click Setup... in the Print dialog box. In the printer setup dialog box, click Setup... and then click Options.... Verify that Printer is selected in the Print To: area, not Encapsulated PostScript.

On occasion a file that has been printed to disk needs to be printed on a Macintosh computer. The following procedure lets you modify the ASCII file.

1. Open the PostScript file in a word-processing program that reads ASCII text.

2. Delete the first and last characters in the file (a filled-in rectangle or square).

3. Be sure to save the file in ASCII format. Some word-processing programs save in a default format that is not ASCII format.

4. You can now download the file from a Macintosh computer to a printer.

Printing on a monochrome printer

Even if you print the final version of a document containing a PhotoStyler image on an imagesetter, you may use a desktop monochrome printer to print proofs of the document. A laser printer can help you determine whether the file will print, check image dimensions, and review overall image detail. Under some circumstances, you may even produce camera-ready pages on a desktop printer and give them to a commercial printer to create printing plates.

Monochrome printers, such as laser printers and imagesetters, use only one color—black—to reproduce images. The printer resolution (measured in dots per inch, or dpi) determines the fineness of the output.

Low-resolution printers, such as dot-matrix printers, print images at 30 dpi to 300 dpi. They are of limited value in image processing but can be useful for printing clip art or line art that's been scanned and modified in PhotoStyler.

Medium-resolution printers, such as laser printers, print at 300 dpi to 600 dpi. These are low-cost means to proof images. Because laser printers are toner-based, they have more trouble printing grays than printers that can print to optical film. If you're printing final output to paper on a medium-resolution desktop printer, a screen frequency of 85 lpi or lower is preferable.

Higher resolution desktop printers, with output at 600 dpi and higher, offer better-quality proof output than medium-resolution laser printers. These printers can create camera-ready paper output if you are producing images for newsprint-quality paper stock or photocopiers.

Before you print, you must install a printer in Windows and select a Precision Transform through the KODAK PRECISION Color Management System. If you are proofing your publication on one printer but intend to print the final version on another printer, you need to install both printers in Windows.

To print grayscale output from a color image, choose Grayscale from the Convert To submenu on the Image menu to convert your image to grayscale.

Tip: Print camera-ready pages on acetate to decrease dot gain and improve registration quality. The acetate doesn't stretch as much as paper when film is created.

Printing color separations

Most full-color printing processes produce color images by first separating the electronic image into four grayscale images called color separations. Each separated image corresponds to one of the four printing inks: cyan, magenta, yellow, or black. The images are printed one on top of another using their corresponding inks, producing the full-color image.

You will usually want color separations only when using commercial printing. If you are creating color separations, you can have PhotoStyler or the printer driver determine the separation options; ask your service provider which method works best.

The Precision Transform (PT) you select through the KODAK PRECISION Color Management System (CMS) has predetermined values for many separations settings based on the final output type: screen frequency, screen angle, dot gain, total ink limit, under color removal (UCR), gray component replacement (GCR), and other settings. These settings are designed to produce the best output on specific paper stock for the final output device.

If your service provider requests specific UCR and GCR values, you can view the PT to see if it has the desired settings. If it does not, you can check related PTs for the settings. If the settings requested aren't available, you may want to contact Kodak about the availability of other PTs or ask the provider to change the settings on the press.

For more information on selecting a PT for your final output type, see "Selecting a Precision Transform for final output" on page 80.

You can select from two options in the Separations section of the Options dialog box: By PhotoStyler and By Printer and Use Printer's Defaults. Selecting By PhotoStyler gives PhotoStyler control over all the separations settings listed above. Selecting By Printer and Use Printer's Defaults gives the printer driver control over all separations settings except orientation. Select this option to use non-Aldus printer drivers, which may have additional options.

Use PhotoStyler options for Negative and emulsion side instead of the Mirror or Negative Image options in the Graphics section of the Advanced Options dialog box in Windows PostScript printer setup. Selecting the Windows options may decrease performance.

To print separations directly from PhotoStyler

1. Verify that both the current and the final printers are set up correctly. For more information, see "Working with proofing and final printers" on page 82.

2. Choose Print… from the Print submenu on the File menu. In the Print dialog box, make sure the CMYK: 4 Pages option is checked. Specify additional printing options in the Print and Options dialog boxes if necessary.

3. Click OK to print the separations.

To prepare an image for separation from another application

1. Choose CMYK True Color from the Convert To submenu on the Image menu.

2. The CMS prompts you to select the final output device in the Select Output Device dialog box. If you need to view the specifics of the output device's Precision Transform, you can click the Color Configure… button and choose Output… from the View menu. Click OK to accept the selected output device.

3. PhotoStyler preseparates the image file. The file contains separation information for each process color.

4. Place the PhotoStyler image in another application that accepts CMYK information. The application reads the separation information included in the image file. The final output device of the application must be the same as the final output device you specified in PhotoStyler for the separations to print correctly.

Optimizing an image for video display

When your final output remains on the screen, you don't need to convert your PhotoStyler image to CMYK format. RGB color format is preferable.

For on-screen output, your chief concerns are the size and resolution of your image and its display on a computer monitor.

Match image resolution to screen resolution to improve screen redraw and reduce file size. A resolution of 25 to 72 dpi is often adequate for displaying images in desktop presentation programs.

A video card installed in your computer determines the number of colors that can be displayed on your computer monitor. If you want to display 24-bit images on screen, a 24-bit video card is recommended to display all 16.7 million colors possible. If your video card is standard VGA, you can display only 16 colors. In this case, it is best to convert PhotoStyler images that will be displayed on the screen to 16-color images. Converting to a 16-color image deletes color data.

Displaying PhotoStyler images in desktop presentation programs

Desktop presentation programs, such as Aldus Persuasion, let you place a PhotoStyler image directly into a presentation.

If the video card installed in the computer you use for on-screen presentations displays only 16 or 256 colors, convert PhotoStyler images to indexed 16-color or 256-color images before placing them in the presentation program.

Find out whether the desktop presentation program you're working with can place 24-bit TIFF images. The desktop presentation program may require you to place an image in the file or may require you to link the image. Aldus Persuasion links any bitmap larger than 57K.

Microsoft PowerPoint version 3.0 does not give you the option to link images and will include the bitmap image as part of the file.

It may be helpful to store linked presentation images on a removable hard drive. For more information on removable hard drives, see "File storage and transfer" on page 70.

If you will also be using the images in 35mm slide presentations, you may need to prepare an additional version of the image for the different output format. For more information, see "Printing on a film recorder" on page 92.

Displaying a PhotoStyler image at high resolution in Persuasion

Aldus Persuasion 2.1 displays bitmap images at high resolution (the resolution depends on the video card installed) in slide show mode. However, to conserve disk space in slide view mode, the program displays images at low resolution. If you want to view your images at high resolution during slide view mode as well as during slide shows, you need to add a line to your ALDUS.INI file. In the [Persuasion] section of ALDUS.INI, type in HiResTIFF=1.

Displaying PhotoStyler images in video and multimedia

Using PhotoStyler images in video and multimedia often requires working with 16 or 256 colors for the entire presentation. If you are working with this requirement, you can map the colors in your images to predefined color tables or create color tables specific to your images.

To map images to a predefined color table

1. Choose Indexed 16-Color or Indexed 256-Color from the Convert To submenu on the Image menu to convert the RGB image to an indexed 16-color or 256-color image.

2. Choose Color Table... from the View menu.

3. Click Load... to open a predefined color palette. Check Matching Existing Color in the Load Color Palette File dialog box to match the colors in the image most closely with the selected palette. You can also edit the color table to create a color table specific to your images.

4. Click Preview to see the effect of the color table on the image. Click Save... to save the color table when you are satisfied with the effect.

Printing on a film recorder

You may output your PhotoStyler image on slide film.

To create slides, you print on a film recorder or have a slide service bureau print on a film recorder for you. The film recorder converts a PhotoStyler image into slide format.

Film recorders generate color in a similar manner to computer monitors, so colors you see on your monitor will be closely matched by colors in a slide. Keep your image as an RGB TIFF; don't convert to CMYK to output to a film recorder.

Because of the way slide film is created, image file sizes can be extremely large. Slide film is read (recorded) vertically. Standard 35mm formats are 2K, 4K, and 8K, or 2000, 4000, and 8000 lines per inch. The more lines per inch, the more data, the larger the file, the more time it takes to record the image, and the higher the quality.

To ensure that the image has the optimal detail for slide output, you need to know its final size. For more information, see "Scanning an image" on page 58.

If you will also be using the image in printed material, you may need to prepare an additional version of the image for the different output format.

Because film recorder drivers are mostly device-specific, they may require different setup procedures and react differently with PhotoStyler. Not all film recorders have drivers for Windows; your driver may be supplied by your film recorder or may be provided by another company. For more information, see your film recorder driver documentation.

Questions to ask a slide service bureau

- Can they work with the format you require (35mm or 4-by-5-inch transparency)?
- How do they receive the large file sizes that film recorder output requires?
- Do they accept files from PCs?
- Are they familiar with Windows-based applications?
- How do they handle aspect ratios that vary from the 3:2 standard?
- What is the resolution of the film recorder they use (in lpi)?

To prepare an image for printing on a film recorder

1. Choose Printer Setup... from the Print submenu on the File menu.

2. Click Setup... in the Printer Setup dialog box for the film recorder you have selected and select the settings you want.

3. The options that are available will be specific to the driver you have installed.

Printing duotone images in PhotoStyler

A duotone is a halftone printed in two colors. Traditionally, a duotone is created as a two-color halftone reproduction of a black-and-white image, with a dark color printed at the standard 45-degree screen angle for black-and-white images and a lighter color printed at a screen angle 30 degrees from the first.

To create a standard duotone effect for printing on a commercial press, follow the procedure listed here. This procedure uses grayscale images, not 24-bit color images, to produce the duotone effect. Because different combinations of plates and colors produce different duotone effects, you will want to work with your service provider as you create the duotone plates.

To create a standard duotone effect when printing

1. Choose Duplicate... from the Edit menu or press Ctrl + D twice to create two duplicates of the grayscale image for which you want to create a duotone effect. Close the original image.

2. Make sure the first duplicate has normal contrast. Reduce the highlights in the image. This image becomes the black plate when it is printed.

3. Increase the contrast and highlights for the second duplicated image. This image will become the second color plate. Work with your print shop to determine the amount to reduce highlights for the first duplicate or increase contrast for the second duplicate.

4. Choose Options... from the Print submenu on the File menu. Click By PhotoStyler in the Halftone section of the Options dialog box.

5. Select the first duplicate image and choose Print... from the Print submenu on the File menu. Set Halftone Angle to 45 degrees in the Output section of the Print dialog box. Click OK to print the image.

6. Select the second duplicate image and choose Print... from the Print submenu on the File menu. Set the Halftone Angle to 75 degrees in the Output section of the Print dialog box. Click OK to print the image.

7. Give the two pictures to your commercial printer, explaining what spot color to add to the second plate. The effect of the combined plate is a toned, or duotone, image.

Index